THE
core
OF
TEACHING

THE *core* OF TEACHING

Experiences and relationships that transformed my life as a teacher

LETICIA RAMOS, M.Ed.

Copyright © 2020 Leticia Ramos

All rights reserved. No part of this publication may be reproduced, distributed, or transmitted in any form or by any means, including photocopying, recording, or other electronic or mechanical methods, without the prior written permission of the publisher, except in the case of brief quotations embodied in reviews and certain other noncommercial uses permitted by copyright law.

Paperback ISBN: 978-1-7349837-0-8
Ebook ISBN: 978-1-7349837-1-5

EDU032000   EDUCATION / Leadership
SEL021000   SELF-HELP / Motivational & Inspirational
OCC019000   BODY, MIND & SPIRIT / Inspiration & Personal Growth

Cover design by Lisa Barbee
Typeset by Kaitlin Barwick

To my mother, who always told me I could do whatever my heart desired.

To my husband, Roger—thank you for telling me that I could and that I should!

I love you!

Contents

Introduction 1

Chapter One: My Great Lesson 7
Chapter Two: Doing the Extra 13
Chapter Three: The Three Cs 17
Chapter Four: Lead with Love 27
Chapter Five: A Full Heart 35
Chapter Six: Working through the Struggles 43
Chapter Seven: Courage to Write 51
Chapter Eight: My Fourth-Grade Teacher, Mr. Anderson 59
Chapter Nine: Leaving Our Legacy 65
Chapter Ten: Inspiration 75
Chapter Eleven: Mr. "O" 81
Chapter Twelve: Cultivating Gratitude 91

Acknowledgments 95
About the Author: Leticia Ramos 99

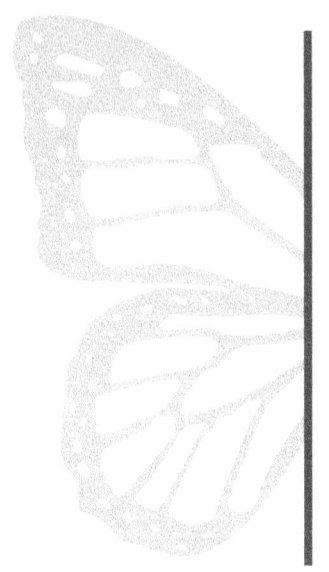

Introduction

INTRODUCTION

Dear Future Teacher,

The essence of teaching is more complex than most can even imagine. I have worked tirelessly to inspire my own students to work toward goals that will create extraordinary results, not just at school but at home as well. Often, the role of a teacher is not just to "teach" but also to be a psychologist, a special friend, an office worker, a coach, a mentor—and the list goes on. For most, a teacher is a person who cares enough to instill good values in others so that they can continue to make a difference in this world and in the life of others.

Have you ever stopped to ask yourself what drove you or inspired you to take the educational path as a career? As I move through my teaching career, I have considered this question and have often thought about the people that influenced me to embrace my teaching journey and work to my fullest potential.

I can tell you that I have often stopped to ponder about whether I am doing the right thing. Many times, I sit with myself and wonder about where I am at in my career. I have questioned whether I am living up to my potential as a teacher and entertaining the highest level of creativity and rigor with my students. The job of a teacher requires an endless amount of effort, risk, patience, collaboration, and a list of never-ending tasks to complete in a classroom.

Some of the content I've written in this book comes from previous experiences. As I began my writing journey, the process for writing my book took a different turn. I would like to caution you at the beginning: Don't expect to be in this profession for the money and the lavish life you can live while teaching. What you *can* expect is to receive an abundance of love, smiles welcoming you daily, enthusiasm from your students, and great satisfaction when you see the progress your students make. Student success becomes possible because a teacher like you and me had at least something (if not a lot) to do with them reaching milestones in their educational journey and getting a sense of accomplishment along the way. Celebrating student successes is one of the greatest benefits of being a teacher.

I don't have any published books and I have never been asked to give a TED talk, nor have I impacted a mass population on social media, but perhaps my book will have an influence on you. As a teacher for over twenty years and working in the personal development field for almost ten years, I have noticed many teachers often seek to find greater things in their careers that fill their life with joy. My intent is to inspire others to do greater things and let you know that this world needs more teachers that are willing to change up the game and drive through the education field with love, courage, passion, and purpose.

In my teaching career, I have done countless things that failed, but one thing I know is that you can't have success without failure. I have learned to appreciate my failures because I understand that failure and success go hand in hand. The notion of failure has been the bully that stares me down and makes me feel uncomfortable, but I have learned not to dwell on the struggles that led me to fail or come close to failure. Instead, I am willing to commit to what I can deliver and treat my failures as opportunities to create changes in my environment and in the classroom.

One of the changes that occurred to me was to invest time in personal development training and in mindfulness practices that gave me new tools for evolving as a teacher. In my training, I developed new friendships with people who inspired and taught me. I learned how to train myself to practice, how to be and how to live through new habits of success. One of the things I was dedicated to doing was studying successful leaders and teachers. I studied the work of Jack Canfield, Dr. Brené Brown, Dr. Wayne Dyer, and Oprah Winfrey. It's vital that teachers make time to care for themselves and receive adequate training that nurtures the mental and physical requirements for them to be great in their profession. Our students need teachers who have the energy, desire, and mental health to continue in the profession.

Learning new habits of success was a quest that often challenged me. If I wanted my students to have the best teacher, it was important that I worked from a higher summit and stayed outside my comfort zone. I was committed to doing things for the first time even if I failed or wasn't content with my results. One valuable tool I used consistently that got me back onto the right path was to think about how I could be the cause for people to feel better about themselves or want to improve their life. I wondered how I could serve my students and colleagues better. The questions that still stay with me, that I often think about, are "Am I showing up to work as the best version of myself today?" and "How do I cultivate relationships that matter with my students and colleagues?"

One question I ask my students is this: "How can we all be part of the challenges we faced today in our classroom and see them as great rewards for us?" I am amazed by the answers my students give, and I am always willing to learn from them through conversations and their actions. Some of my students understand that mistakes are part of the journey to learning something new. Sometimes this is difficult for them to understand. Having a constantly reflective mindset worked well for me and allowed me to be part of the solution to many challenges I faced in my teaching career. I wish I had learned earlier what I know now because I would have been able to use the tools that lead to extraordinary results sooner.

Today, I am learning to focus on aligning my thoughts with my deepest passions and being intentional with all that I do, both in my classroom and in my personal life. I am constantly evolving as a teacher and my classroom has been a gateway to being part of more than just a learning community, but also a melting pot where many friendships are made through different cultures, where respect and love is the norm.

From my experience, I know that most people do not find 100 percent joy in their jobs, especially in teaching. In fact, most teachers leave within the first three to five years in this profession. There were times when I said I would look for another job, perhaps one that paid more, one that allowed me to work from home or travel and had better benefits than my current job. I bet this thought has crossed your mind too.

I will be using the word "core" a lot in this book, and you will discover new ways in which this word may resonate with you. "Core" simply means to get real and get raw with your feelings, ideas, and beliefs. "Getting down to the core" means to say it out loud without caring about what people think. I challenge you to give yourself permission to do what you need to move on and make the best out of your teaching career and remember why you chose this path.

Being a second-grade teacher has been a privilege, and some of the greatest times I have experienced in life were inside my classroom. The overwhelming love, wisdom, and feedback I have been given from my students have kept me focused on my goals and given me the courage to continue climbing to the top. It has been my students who have touched me and inspired me to do the things that were not going to be possible—and I made them possible! It has been my mission to work as a leader in my field and be a greater contribution for young people and help them thrive to be exceptional in the world.

My students have filled my heart with love, have given me hope, and have made my years of teaching that much richer. They have challenged me to think about questions that call for reflection and

INTRODUCTION

constant pondering. I am humbled by their ability to make me learn more about myself and my job. In this book, my intent is to tell you that young people can have an infinite amount of inspiration and be one of the biggest motivators you can have. I believe I was born to teach, provide great learning opportunities to kids, and be inspired by my students. My journey as a life-long learner continues and I will continue paving the path to an incredible road that leads to bigger ideas and creating relationships that hold great value and are worth nurturing. Today can be the start of a new day for you. I invite you to think about how you are showing up to work every day and impacting the lives of your students. I've been told by mentors and some of my former teachers that when I put my whole heart into what I do and acknowledge the impact I am making on others, I am increasing the probability of getting to where I really want to be or fulfilling new accomplishments in life.

Today I share with you that the time has come. I have re-committed to doing things differently and pursue my dream of writing and expanding what I do now as a teacher and increase my awareness of mastering new things that will add value in my life. I will be one teacher writing to hopefully inspire you to write your own story about what captured your heart and spirit during your teaching years. Getting to the core of what makes your job special and allowing yourself to think about the moments that impacted you the most in your career allows you to acknowledge the beauty of this profession. Maybe you will let us know about the most beautiful moments you had as a teacher or how you reached moments of inspiration in your career. I invite you to let your ideas flow and your mind to wander so that you can grant us permission to be captivated by your words and experiences. Share your wisdom and make a difference in the life of another human being by simply being your best self. Show up and tell!

Chapter One

My Great Lesson

CHAPTER ONE: MY GREAT LESSON

There are times when I take a moment to observe my students interact and work diligently on their assignments. As I observe them having conversations with each other, I wonder what they are feeling or thinking about. My thoughts are usually that they are happy learning in my classroom, excited about what is to come, and willing to be brave enough to take on new learning challenges without feeling apprehensive.

As a teacher, I have been in situations where my students arrived at school and *looked* ready to start their day. However, their appearance was a mask; I was fooled by their appearance and what it said about their preparedness and needs. There have been times when my students' primary needs, such as sleep or having enough to eat, were not being met. It's difficult to teach students under those circumstances because oftentimes teachers do not always know what life at home for a student is like. When I encounter situations like this, I find myself taking on a different role than just a teacher. I suddenly became like a caretaker or the nurturing mother.

On occasions I have given my students a toothbrush so they could tend to their dental hygiene or I allowed extra bathroom time so they could wash their face and run their little fingers through their hair so they looked presentable at the start of the school day.

My eyes haven't always seen the prettiest illustration of a healthy and happy student. There have been times when my students come to school and perhaps their last meal was the school lunch they had the day before. I have been surprised by the strength some students display and how some can actually still make it through a school day on very little sleep and nourishment. The resiliency a child displays is remarkable and truly something I think we can all emulate.

In my experience, I have learned that if I want to establish a healthy and safe environment for my students, I need to be compassionate and understanding toward their needs. Working with young kids means to be on the lookout for signs of hardships they may be encountering. Students can arrive at school with problems or feeling sad or distracted, and sometimes they make efforts to mask how they really feel, which has made it harder for me to understand them and help them.

Many times, they won't acknowledge what they truly feel because of fear. That fear can be displayed and manifested in many ways. As teachers it is important to take caution on how we do things in school. For me, it's important to be intentional about how I spend time with them. Thinking about my purpose for doing things is valuable because I have learned that when I do things with purpose, I have better results in reaching my students and meeting not only their primary needs but also their learning needs. As a teacher, I strive hard to expose my students to the notion of articulating how they feel and encourage them to tell what they need from me in order to feel successful and happy.

One year when I was teaching second grade, I had a student who always had a warm attitude toward other students. This little boy was kind and compassionate and a great friend. He was well liked and often invited to play with other playground buddies. He ran and played without a care in the world. I will use the name Adam to illustrate the scenario.

One day we were working on a classroom project where we were studying animal habitats. Students began to describe their own living areas—their homes. When it was Adam's turn, he drew certain pictures about his home environment that included a trash can,

CHAPTER ONE: MY GREAT LESSON

a wooden floor, a park, and a bus. Some students were beginning to think he didn't understand the lesson. While some kids were struggling to figure out what Adam was describing, he decided to tell the entire class about his work.

Adam bravely stood in front of the class as he began to explain. The trash cans from the city park were places his mother would search for extra food to feed the family. The brown floor was the color of the rug he slept on because he didn't have a bed. The park was the place where his mother would take them to collect cans after their homework was done and, if they were lucky, also to have somebody's leftovers. The bus was how they would get around because his family did not own a car. His mother and father owned bicycles, but most of the time they walked or used public transportation.

I learned a huge lesson from that experience. Adam taught me to look for the good in everything even when life gets tough. It was through his resilience that I understood life is a game and how I play it matters. My eyes filled with tears; my heart ached for this student and his family. I wanted to hug him and tell him, *I wish I could take it all away*. Adam told us that going to the park was fun because his parents gave him time to play and he and his siblings would see who could collect the most cans. It was just like when they say, "When life gives you lemons, make lemonade." Adam was a great example of what wearing a resilient mask looked like because he showed up daily with enthusiasm and was eager to start his day. Adam was always willing to do more even though he had very little. His kind gestures in the classroom went a long way. He was helpful and always willing to take on and do more.

A short time after this incident, I was approached by a woman after school who stated she was Adam's mother. I had never seen his mother and father because I had not been successful at having a parent-teacher conference with them. She explained their home environment to me and told me about their financial limitations and the family challenges they had encountered. I would have never known these details because Adam was responsible with his work, arrived on time, and was so carefree.

Adam's mother was the same lady I used to see looking through the trash cans the year before as I walked with my class to the city library. Sometimes she already had a few bags in her hand and she would not only get cans but what seemed to be food scraps. I was crushed. It saddened me to learn about Adam's family's story, his home environment, and his living conditions. Adam had very little, but he valued his education, he loved being in school, never complained, and managed to do well academically. His perspective on life made a huge impact on me and seeing the way he made time in his day to be happy and make the best out of his living situation was admirable.

Many times, our students are our greatest teachers, masters of cultivating and enriching learning experiences for us and geniuses at intelligently showing us how to live, learn, and being our best selves. Poverty is a giant hurdle to cross, but that didn't stop Adam from excelling in school and being a perfect example of finding the good in every situation.

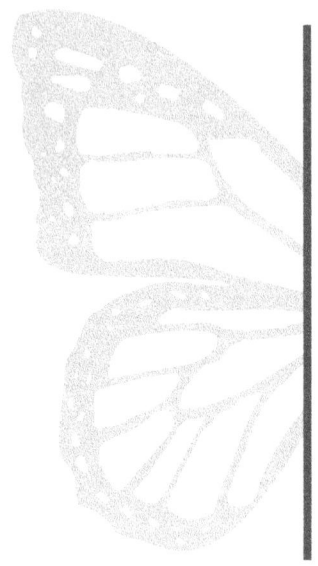

Chapter Two

Doing the Extra

CHAPTER TWO: DOING THE EXTRA

Changes can show up in our learning environment in an instant, and teachers are often faced with the challenge to act upon them quickly. Aside from our daily job assignments, we are constantly presented with meeting different students' needs and caring for our students because sometimes they arrive at school unprepared.

Some teachers work long hours, attend extra curricular events on weekends and go the extra mile for their students. These teachers are the extraordinary ones, the ones I like to call the game-changers! They make the impossible possible and open up new possibilities for their students. These teachers are in constant growth, creating and learning about the latest educational programs and trends.

I recently learned about an amazing woman who went the extra mile for her students, her district, and her community. Linda Cliatt-Wayman was a principal from Strawberry Mansion High School in the Philadelphia School District. Strawberry Mansion High was considered a dangerous school. Most students there at the time Principal Cliatt-Wayman was principal were struggling academically and there was a high dropout rate.

This brave principal stepped up to a vicious challenge and turned things around for that high school. At first, Principal Cliatt-Wayman volunteered to become principal of Strawberry Mansion High because nobody else was willing to take the job. With the help of her staff and other members of the community, she worked diligently to create a major plan to convert the school and change the students' philosophy about their education. Most of the students didn't care and often preferred to be elsewhere. Because her students and the school were surrounded by poverty, the first thing she did was clean out the school. She reallocated funds so that new teachers and support staff could be on campus not only to supervise but also to mentor students, as well as to purchase furniture and new materials. She made sure the school walls were displayed with motivational messages and that the educational program was modified in order to meet the academic, emotional, and social needs of students. Strawberry Mansion went through a major transformation thanks to Principal Cliatt-Wayman. She was the champion and force students needed in order to have educational breakthroughs and begin to feel a sense of accomplishment and self-worth.

Principal Cliatt-Wayman's story stood out to me because I have worked for a school district where some students and their families have also experienced financial and economic hardships. Most of the students who struggled academically at the elementary level never finished high school and some are on a slow path to reach that milestone. In my teaching community, some students have little or no support at home, and some parents never had formal schooling after high school.

Despite the circumstances I faced in my classroom, I found it necessary to stay in teaching and be the best imaginable role model for my students. This job wasn't always easy, and I faced many struggles trying to accomplish this task. There were times when I felt that it was time to pursue another endeavor and focus on something new. But when I stopped to analyze how I impacted my students and how much they added to my life, I knew I had to continue teaching. By staying in the teaching field, I had another opportunity to create an environment where we all learned from each other and had a sense of belonging. I could be the person who would love my students without fear and could acknowledge them for developing amazing relationships that nurtured learning, risk taking, exploring, and staying committed to learning even if we encountered struggles and made mistakes along the way.

Sometimes when I faced challenging times in my classroom and had to take on multiple roles as a teacher, I would think back to the beautiful witty smile that greeted me as Adam walked into my classroom—excited and without a care in the world, ready for the day. Many times teachers are not prepared for unforeseen circumstances that are out of our control. Teachers just make things happen and sometimes we don't know how but we do. When our actions are driven by love, passion, and commitment to our job and what we stand for, we can all achieve more.

The following quote reminds me of Principal Cliatt-Wayman's amazing act of service and love for her high school.

> "Nobody cares how much you know, until they know how much you care."
>
> —Theodore Roosevelt

Principal Cliatt-Wayman was a perfect example of what it is to do more, to lead, and to give kids hope. I wonder what the education profession would be like if we had more individuals like Linda. When I first learned about Principal Cliatt-Wayman's story, I was inspired to do more. I wanted to reach not only more students but also more teachers and to let them know we need to continue striving to be better role models for our students and consistently work as beacons of promoting excellence and exceptional learning practices. When we do more, we are selflessly doing greater things for our students and making a greater educational impact on them. When I have been in the forefront to give the extra for my students, they know how much I care and always will.

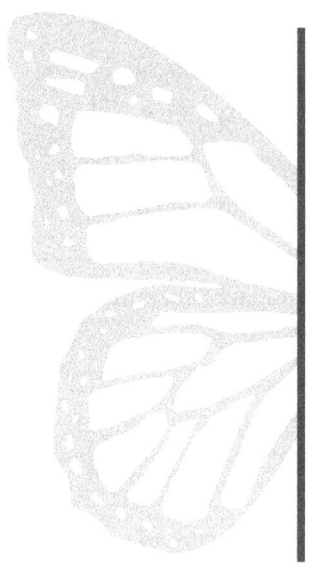

Chapter Three

The Three Cs

CHAPTER THREE: THE THREE CS

One day I found myself sitting in a professional development workshop feeling anxious and uneasy. As I glanced around the room from the hard, wooden seat I was sitting on, I could see the room was quickly filling with teachers who probably felt like me—like I had something better to do on a Saturday morning. Sometimes I had a sense of guilt kick in on weekends because I was away from my family to attend another professional development training.

I stood there for a moment, and instead of allowing myself to become angry, I welcomed patience and being open-minded about my day. I sat there patiently waiting for the coffee line to shorten before I made my way there and I poured myself one.

Then our facilitator made his entrance. He gracefully and slowly made his way toward the front of the room. He was tall, had long hair, and was wearing Birkenstocks, plain worn-in jeans, and a checkered flannel shirt. He certainly did not look like the facilitators I was used to having in workshops because most facilitators dressed in business attire.

The facilitator introduced himself as Jim, and he had infectious enthusiasm. Jim looked like he was in total bliss, excited to be in our space and start his day. He cracked a few jokes and shared a few slides before we began our icebreaker activity. There was *something* about him. At first I struggled to figure it out. His energy and delivery were transparent and inviting. I was beginning to think that we weren't going to stay in our seats because he had props around the room.

After a few minutes of chatting and greeting each other, we started our first exercise and Jim asked us to make a large circle. After a fun way to introduce ourselves, the question came: What are you grateful for in your profession? This was a question I didn't hear too often in a professional training for teachers, and although the question was new for me in that space, I knew there was a lot I could be grateful for. Already I knew that this felt different and not like most teacher workshops I attended. Most workshops I attended had to do with State Standards and other learning practices.

But that question profoundly impacted me and the way I think about my life as a teacher. I found myself in deep thought and in search for the perfect answer even though sometimes the perfect answer is not the right answer. I looked around the room and I saw it. I heard it. Teachers shyly answered as if they didn't want anyone to know what they were grateful for. I could see the hesitation to speak from other members of the group, some teachers were reluctant to share and I don't know if it was because they were shy or preferred to keep quiet longer. I heard others say, "Ms. Ramos, your turn, what are you grateful for?" I had been in a deep wander and my thoughts were everywhere.

"Connection." That was the first word that came out of my mouth and I knew that word well, but not in that space. "I am truly humbled by the deep connections and friendships I have made being a teacher," I added. Some people nodded and other group members commented on my answer. One individual told me they were curious about that and asked if I could share a bit more later.

Our trainer asked us to think about our response to his question and that we would revisit it again before the training was over. He went on to add that we already had everything we needed for the day, we were all invited to use ourselves to create the training and do what we could to make it memorable and meaningful. I was a bit confused and couldn't understand what he meant by that. He went on to say that we would be working in smaller groups and would have an opportunity to lead in our groups just like inside our classrooms. Teachers lead every day in territories we are familiar with and with the same teams. That day, we were invited to take action moments and lead within our small groups and create opportunities to connect with new people.

Our experiential exercises continued, and I could tell that teachers and principals were really digging this training just like me. I was willing to do the work, be an active participant, and lead in our group. I could tell that, as the day progressed, more teachers were becoming more comfortable and willing to initiate during activities, share, and often lead our group into a new direction. We never knew where we would end up, and the journey getting there meant we had to support each other in various ways to meet our goals for the day and collaborate and even think outside the box. Our trainer told us to think about how our everyday actions affect others in our work environment and our students in our classrooms.

As we left for our lunch break, we were told we would have a working lunch and would need to answer some questions that pertained to our current status in the teaching field. Right away, there were people in my group who said they weren't getting paid to work during their lunch, so they opted out of the exercise while a few were still willing and cooperative. I was one of the members who willingly opted to proceed with the exercises and took the lead.

Soon after we sat down, one person stated that he felt vulnerable when the first question came about teaching. He mentioned that he has never really thought about it wholeheartedly because one thing he knew was that our profession wasn't the best paying job but he rather enjoyed the time off during the summers. Today, however, he had a moment to ponder and digest the question in order to derive an honest answer. I stated what I had mentioned earlier in the morning, "I am grateful for the connections and **learning** that I receive in my class and at school. If we allow ourselves to be open to anything for that particular day, we can learn so much even from our students. Then again, if we close ourselves off, the learning process can be minimal. I love to learn from my students and sometimes their inquisitive questions challenge me at finding an answer or creating an opportunity to explore certain topics further." My students are indispensable in my life because at the end of the day we make time to have a mindful moment to think about our gains for that day. I accomplish a great deal in those last five minutes of our school day and what they share holds a great deal of value. These are mini lessons I look forward to and appreciate how sometimes unplanned conversations create a magical flow of questions and inquiry among my students. Sometimes these small chats leave us desiring more time to connect and we have to refer back to that at a later time.

According to the Oxford dictionary, "learning" is described as follows:

> learn·ing
> /ˈlər–niŋ/
> noun
> 1. the acquisition of knowledge or skills through experience, study, or by being taught

Learning is a process that we all partake in from the minute we are born. Learning fuels me, energizes me, and challenges me. Learning can take form in many ways we just have to be willing to accept it and nurture it so it grows. I was definitely learning a lot from conversations we were having. I realized there are many wonderful people in the teaching field and making a huge impact in the lives of their students.

We continued working and quickly moved through the exercise because our time was almost done. This was the perfect opportunity to come clean and unravel the truth. The truth that maybe exposed my vulnerability to others. I had kept some thoughts to myself and never shared them with others. I had read an article that mentioned more teachers were making career changes because they couldn't keep up with the demands of teaching. Another topic I spoke about was that while teacher shortages are real, I felt that if teachers were trained more on mental health, teacher wellbeing, and mindfulness practices to support students with traumas and other social emotional issues they could be experiencing, then our teachers would stay in the field and continue to lead inside the classrooms.

That morning was filled with humbling chats over how teachers have been impacted by their job. Some members shared tears; there were hugs and laughter. As I looked around the room, I was embraced by warmth and caring thoughts from other members that were sharing about our profession. Some had been in their field for over 40 years and were finally retiring, while others had only just begun their teaching journey and already felt like they were ready to throw in the towel. The realization that more teachers are leaving the profession saddened me.

As people cross our paths and observe our moments with them, we may discover a valuable lesson. Sometimes we must just take time to observe and let our internal voice tell us what we need to know. As I ventured about my day, I sought to find the lessons left behind from other members in my training, especially the people in my small lunch group.

As the training went on, I was very mindful about what we were doing, and paid close attention to what our facilitator was saying.

While doing another exercise, we were all told to take a card and read it. My card said:

> "What three words would you
> use to describe your job?"

"Collaboration," "compassion," and "caring" were words that stood out in my mind because as individuals in this world, it is important to be in constant collaboration and care for people who share our world, our working environment, our team, and our home. For me, it has been important to nurture the idea of having compassion for my students, caring, and contributing to support them in time of need. Showing compassion for students allows them to have a sense of safety and trust in me. Compassion can bring people together, increase student engagement, and reduce levels of stress and frustration.

As a teacher, I often think about the following question: How can you lead the younger minds to a path of success and inquiry without caring about what you do? Why would you expect your students to show up every day, learn everything, and stay on task when you probably were not committed to your goals that day? It's not fair to wake up, go to work, and set out for the day without preparation and expect our students to give us extraordinary results if we are not working at our best. I know there are times when I put myself and my needs last and allow myself to get caught up in other things. Teachers need to care for ourselves first, to feed our soul with what soothes us and gives us a boost of good energy. This is part of the core of teaching. I make time to practice yoga, meditate, and keep a journal to help me focus on my thoughts and boosts my mood.

Teaching allows me to share what I know with others. It is a platform for letting others know I care, and possibly even opening up a moment for vulnerability and compassion. Authentic and honest contribution leads to the root of caring for others and being willing to exchange your thoughts to receive someone else's. It means to put yourself into a space where you can be heard from your weakest, saddest, most joyful, angriest, and most excited moments. Those are just a few to say the least; however, as a constant collaborator and receiver of wisdom, I know my growth will never stop because I plan to place myself in a space where I am an important variable for the younger generation.

We moved into our last exercise and we were all told to make a huge circle and face inward. The facilitator asked us to look at the teachers from our school and think of one positive thing we could say about each member. He asked us to think about how we can all do one great thing for one another and create a magical year for all. Before the first teacher began, there were tears of gratitude and appreciation, warmth from the teachers that just by the looks you could feel the love and admiration. I must say, this exercise has been one of the most impactful and fulfilling exercises I have been a part of with my colleagues. Teachers let their guards down, took off their stoic masks, and allowed themselves to be however they needed to be to make the exercise beneficial and true, even if that meant being vulnerable.

Vulnerability was present in the room. Our hearts were full, and we felt ready to conquer the job and all the challenges that came along with it. We all convened in the circle we started with. Our faces looked different; some teachers had tears, some had smiles, and some teachers acknowledged each other with a nod and smile from across the room. We ended our training with a big thank-you hug and some teachers were still taking it all in. Gratitude conversations led right into reflection and small group talk.

When you give yourself an opportunity to reach out and contribute in a way that matters and impacts another member from your teaching staff, you will be surprised what you create for yourself and that person. All it takes is a second to change another person's day; sometimes it's with a smile, a greeting in the morning, or a compliment as you both start your day, going out of your way to help others and simply being present in the moment. Contributing with caring thoughts and respect can go a long way and you can make a difference. Caring about another person means you have taken time to value yourself enough to leave a mark in their life and create a special feeling of admiration for them.

Our gratitude conversation came to an end, and I felt like I didn't want the training to end. It was a truly amazing experience to share, collaborate, and be in constant communication with other teachers who also had a huge commitment with kids. Having conversations that are heartfelt, reflective and allow me to think about what my next steps for creating extraordinary learning experiences for my students is something worth sharing. I learn a tremendous amount when I collaborate with colleagues, especially when we have similar interests or goals. I loved the training and only wish more teachers could be part of something so rewarding and great.

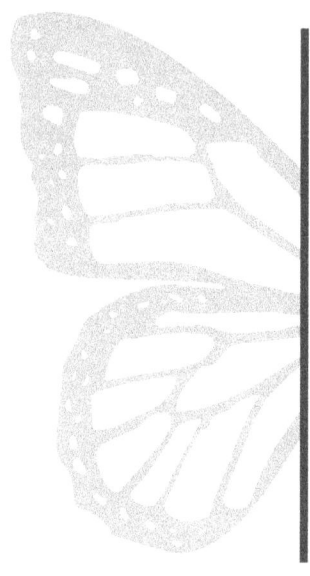

Chapter Four

Lead with Love

CHAPTER FOUR: LEAD WITH LOVE

I have been blessed to have been able to stand in front of a young audience for the past twenty-two years and develop creative ways to teach math, reading, writing, and other subjects that are required by the state of California. I often found myself in constant growth, learning from others and through workshops; being the teacher I am today took patience, making mistakes, and being okay with that, knowing that what I did one day would matter.

I have been through numerous workshops, had different mentors, and been part of pilot-based programs. I have learned that building relationships with students is key to having a successful year. This idea has been challenging at times. Nevertheless, I have slowly allowed students into my personal life, been open about my likes and dislikes, and shown them who their guide for the year is. My personal life holds my dreams, my biggest fears, my wants, and even a bucket-list that describes my wishes for the years to come. Becoming this teacher wasn't always easy because I have always been a bit reserved with my personal life and have usually kept my professional life strictly professional.

There was a point in my life when I had many obstacles crossing my path and huge lifelong decisions to make. I was trying to start a business while being a full-time teacher. There were times when I felt a sense of burnout and ideas for inspiration were dimming.

Then one day after school I was speaking to my mentor. I remember the question that was addressed to me like it was yesterday. My left shoulder leaned on the hallway wall a couple of feet from my classroom, and I could feel the weight of my bookbag beginning to cause tension on my shoulder. (Those teacher's guides can get pretty heavy, especially when you have two in your bag.) She asked me, "What did you love about your previous teachers? What was it about your junior high or high school teachers that made them special to you?" Those questions took me by surprise because I was never asked that. Suddenly this made me think about my students and what they could possibly say if they were asked the same question about me. Our hallway chat had quickly turned into an hour-long conversation, which led us back into my classroom. It was very easy to describe what those teachers were like and how they impacted my life while going to school.

Our conversation led us both to reflect on how teaching has shifted from years ago because learning styles differ greatly now. Perhaps my teachers gave me what I needed at the time or simply worked to be the best role models and showed actions of love and respect. I was suddenly drawn to elaborating on our conversation and excited to hear more about what her experiences were like and how she was influenced by her teachers.

I grew eager and felt like a student in my classroom waiting to blurt out my answer. I told my mentor the answer in one word: LOVE. My teachers were leaders who had a calling for their job, and I knew they taught with love. There were times when some of my teachers would put their students first before their families or themselves. Some lost sleep and spent countless hours after school and on weekends to support me. As a young student, I couldn't really understand why or how teachers could spend so much time at school, sometimes doing the extra and being my coach, then work on Saturdays and train on Sundays. My teachers were caring, dedicated, passionate, and willing to be a friend to me and others. I felt a sense of closeness to them, and I knew they cared about my future.

CHAPTER FOUR: LEAD WITH LOVE

As teachers, continuing to be soaring maestros in the education field is important and something that needs to be taken seriously. As we plant the seeds of knowledge and tend to young curious minds, we need to be the vital elements that support the academic growth of our students. Challenging ourselves to try to learn new things in education is a great way to expand our awareness to other things that encompass the core of teaching. Sometimes as teachers, we are presented with new positions that call for stepping it up in the hierarchy in the teaching arena. There have been times when I entertained the thought of taking a different position outside the classroom—and on one occasion I did.

I had been looking for new inspiration and was ready for a change in both my personal and professional life. I began to journal and work on designing a new vision board for myself. I decided to expand on my personal goals and implement that process as a lesson inside my classroom with my students. Students beautifully decorated their boards with teachers, dancers, professional athletes, astronauts, firefighters, doctors, fun places of interest, and of course money!

Many times, we instill new ideas, motivate, and give our students countless speeches about working hard, never giving up in school, and doing their best to be great citizens. Sometimes I sound like Tony Robbins. Anthony Robbins is a well-known motivational speaker and life coach. In the classroom, we are like the Tony Robbins for our students and sometimes they love hearing what we have to say. We can spark a new interest or help students find a love for learning something in foreign territory. For that reason, it is important for teachers to make efforts to commit to what we want our students to practice or be like. As a teacher, I can't expect my students to shine and succeed if I am not willing to lead, be the example, and provide opportunities for them to practice and be.

Preaching to my students and giving them my best won't be as effective if I don't live up to my own word and standards.

One day I was tested by a student as we were having a conversation in my class.

I was sitting at the wooden kidney table in the back of the classroom with a group of seven students for writing time. My students were working diligently on their writing projects, and one particular student, Anthony, was an avid writer who often failed to sharpen his pencils because he preferred to keep working and not waste any time and would literally use up the entire lead until the tip was buried deep into the pencil. Many times, I would remind him that his pencils were screaming out for help and needed to be sharpened. This enthusiastic writer never wasted time. His free class time was usually spent on writing stories or making books with beautiful representations of what his wondrous mind held captive. His mind was always on the go, exploring new thoughts and discovering new things about what he learned. He frequently created opportunities for other members of the class to learn along with him and shared something that fascinated him.

We gathered around the table and Anthony was the last to arrive because his mind was occupied on another book for us to read and comment on. The group's conversation went back and forth with the focus on "what makes a good writing piece." I sat there in the middle of the table with my second graders discussing the work of writers and what they would focus on that morning. Before students began to work, I charted the responses to "What makes a good writing piece" and these were the following contributions.

- Good writing has our ideas, best ideas.
- Good writing always shows how we feel or think.
- Good writing makes the reader think.
- Good writing makes you smile, laugh, or cry.

- Good writing can also be bad, sometimes.
- Good writing can make you want to write more, like a book.
- Good writing makes the reader and writer think.
- Good writing makes you brainstorm and it can be messy.
- Good writing can be songs or books like Anthony's . . .

I fell in love with the last bullet point. It was evident that my students understood the significance and value of the work of another classmate. They held high standards for their young classmate and knew his work was so great that his books were just an example of what captured their attention and respect.

Anthony's love for reading and writing grew on them, and he was a true model for others. I smiled and I agreed with the students. I took that moment to give Anthony positive feedback, and my small group did too. Anthony's huge eyelashes flickered in excitement, and when the last student finished, he said, "Thank you for your feedback." And then Anthony looked at me and politely asked, "Ms. Ramos, where is your book? You're a teacher and you say how much you love to read and write . . . how come you haven't written your book?"

Those words hit me like a ton of bricks. My body froze, and I was in deep thought and couldn't answer him. Many things crossed my mind in a matter of seconds. That was exactly what I needed to hear. I never imagined that my eight-year-old second-grade student's words would be the impulse I needed to hear to start thinking about my dream. It's surprising to see how our young students can have a tremendous impact on our dreams and how their words are exactly what we need to hear in order to get the message and be in total alignment with our thoughts and feelings. For a while I had wanted to pursue writing a book and knew I could but it wasn't my priority. I am still in awe by Anthony's comment and am extremely grateful he was in my small group that morning. His love for learning was what allowed him to lead in so many ways. He led me to start moving toward my dream of becoming an author that could inspire others to do something greater, like he did for me!

That day I went home and began to search for a mentor, started going through my old notes, reading my old journal that had my notes titled, "Ms. Ramos—author," and began paging through magazines for inspiration, because my dream to become an author was about to take flight.

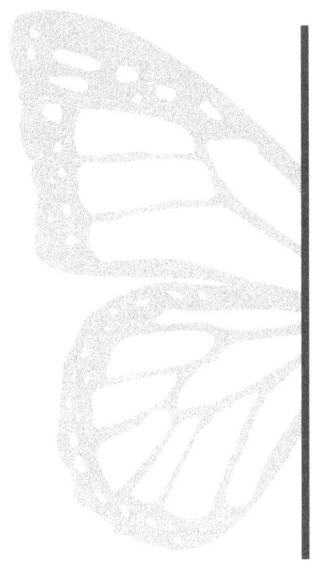

Chapter Five

A Full Heart

CHAPTER FIVE: A FULL HEART

What makes teaching thrilling is when I get to see the looks of joy on my students' faces, the curiosity working through the minds of perplexed students in constant wonder. I love to witness the inquiry unfold before my eyes. I appreciate the intellectual conversations and how they bounce back and forth like a beach ball floating in the air with no direction from student to student. I feel joy when I see lessons being led by young leaders, where new learning challenges are presented by students. It's wonderful to see bright ideas being shared, questions forming from wondering minds about what we learned in class. Listening to the constant sounds of enthusiastic students collaborating, giving feedback, and supporting each other is another dose of excitement because it's evidence that my endless nights of planning and making purposeful lessons has paid off.

When I see my students smile, encourage each other, motivate one another to take a stand, and together cross the line of fear, it assures me that they are on their way to making greater things happen in their personal growth. Having the courage to be heard, to be wrong, to be questioned, and sometimes disagreed with is a huge risk to take. When my students are in constant growth mode and curious minds are in tandem working as a team, I know it's time to change up the game while still nurturing their ideas and contributions. It's gratifying to see what being secure and having comfort looks like and sounds like in room 20: talented young minds working and leaders speaking about their passions and searching for answers and being fine with hitting some bumps along the way. It's truly remarkable to witness the radiating smile of a student who is overjoyed and can't contain themselves with excitement because they have met their goal or demonstrated progress. These are the moments where my young leaders and I have reached another milestone in our education and we celebrate our successes.

I find joy when students hold themselves accountable for their learning. This is something that needs to be taught with care at a young age. Not all our students come from the same backgrounds and socioeconomic status, but that doesn't mean all students can't make it to the top. I remind them to work to their fullest potential because I know they can. For me, the struggle is to make them understand the importance of being accountable and own it. Helping my students see why they matter and that at a very young age they are already contributing to making our world a better place is important.

Have you ever stopped and given yourself time to observe your students? Have you given yourself time to listen attentively to their words, observe their actions, and simply just "be"? As a teacher, I have witnessed and understood that one of the greatest problems teachers face is that they don't listen to what students are saying. Their conversations are invaluable and hold a tremendous amount of worth, and the conversations they own are just as important as yours and mine. It fills me with joy when I see students and teachers holding conversations that are mutually understood, valued, and respected. I started to purposefully take moments throughout my day to reflect upon small conversations that were held in my classroom. I kept a small conversation-gratitude notebook nearby and made a point to annotate something valuable about chats we had throughout the day. Doing this has led to many joyful moments in my day because I have been able to use this exercise as a way to acknowledge the lessons I have received from students. I value and appreciate the small doses of love that were shared. I have been able to use my notes to give my students feedback by leaving them a personal note, writing about it in their notebook or acknowledging them in person. This has led to great writing in my classroom and students wanting to do the same for other students. Doing this frequently in my classroom has allowed students to appreciate each other and the contributions they make.

Being transparent in front of my students is what has allowed me to create an honest, sincere relationship with them. For me, it's important to establish healthy relationships, union, and respect because our second family is at school with our students. That's right folks, teachers and students share a minimum of 180 days out of the year together and for me, having an awesome relationship with my students is necessary. I work repeatedly to create a safe, nurturing, autonomic learning environment in hopes that my students feel comfortable enough to contribute and feel free to be who they want to be every day—and I know there are many more teachers out there who do this better than me!

I am not certain if or when my students will truly understand what they mean to me and how much I value them. These are some of the things I wonder about and reflect upon:

- If my students only knew how much I care about them.
- If my students only knew I worry about them when they go home at the end of the day.
- If my students only knew I appreciate the invaluable lessons they teach me.
- If my students only knew I am so blessed to have them in my class.
- If my students only knew that their actions will affect the future.
- If my students only knew that they can be the next big thing in this world.

- If my students only knew I think they are all truly amazing kids.
- If my students only knew I believe they can all make their huge dreams come true.
- If my students only knew that together, we can make a difference in this world.

Last year I had an awkward situation. I remember when one of my students' seats was empty for two days. I will use the name Joseph. My students were concerned because Joseph was not at school those days. Joseph was tough. He played football and enjoyed his time on the playground with the bigger kids. We knew Joseph's mother had been ill but couldn't figure out why he was absent for two days in a row. Students had their suspicions but the truth of his absence was a mystery.

When Joseph finally arrived, he walked in late and was teary-eyed. Forty-six eyes gazed up at Joseph as he walked through the door and rushed to his seat. I looked at him from the front of the room. I began to worry because I feared something serious was going on with him. Then, it happened so fast, like a flash, quick—and before I knew it Joseph was in his seat. He held up his head and loudly said, "Ms. Ramos, my mom is very sick and she is in the hospital. The ambulance took her during the night, and I don't want her to die!"

I felt the knot in my throat, and could barely hold my tears in. The number 2 pencil in my right hand rolled off onto the table below me and fell on the ground. I made my way over to his seat, but before I could get there, two students had already embraced him with a warm hug. One was a boy and the other a girl. Their little hands could barely reach around Joseph's body and he cried in their arms. His tears slid down his face. The compassion and care the students felt for their classmate was evident. There were tears from other kids who thought of their mothers. Some whispered, "How sad, poor Joseph." Others said, "It's going to be okay, Joseph."

I stood in front of him and gently placed my papers on his desk. I told my students that it meant a lot for me to see how caring and compassionate they were toward their classmate. At that moment, I wasn't sure how Joseph felt about being acknowledged that way, but one thing was clear: my students were vulnerable and brave enough to act on another student's needs regardless of who else was there to see it. My young leaders stepped up to plate and handled their business with the most caring heart. One boy gave Joseph his brand-new travel-size tissue box that was inside his desk. "Here Joseph, keep this and use it when you need it," was what he said. The actions displayed by my students toward Joseph were true and compassionate. I was humbled by the act of care I saw. The love and respect my students displayed for another member of our learning team was an example of transparency taking over. Their compassionate hearts, loving attitudes, and kind spirits radiated throughout the room and were felt by all.

When unexpected things happen, sometimes we are uncertain as to what course of action to take. As teachers, when we repeatedly model positive behavior, when we show how to be compassionate toward others and teach our students about gratitude, love and respect will eventually show up. Doctor Brené Brown speaks repeatedly about the power of vulnerability. As teachers, sometimes our vulnerable moments lead to joy or other beautiful sentiments. It is our duty as teachers to be persistent and work against the fierce current in our classroom that tries to keep us from seeing the good in everything and in people we work with. Over the years, I have learned to embrace my own challenges and learn that it's okay to let myself be vulnerable in front of my students, to love them for who and how they are.

That morning my heart was full, I felt an immense sense of joy because I felt the warmth, love, and compassion my students had for another member of our classroom. I gave Joseph a hug, and he got up out of his seat and he hugged me back. "Thank you, Ms. Ramos. I feel sad for my mom," he said. I told him he was so brave for allowing us to know how he felt and thanked him for letting us help him feel better.

That day Joseph wrote about his mother and the things he was grateful for. He was proud because for the first time he produced a writing piece he was truly proud of. In his writing, he shared that he felt lucky because his classmates loved him and made him feel better. It was a loving message about a strong woman fighting to stay strong, to recover so she could go to her son's football games again without an oxygen tank. He asked if he could take his writing home to show his mother when he visited her in the hospital that afternoon.

As a teacher, I have witnessed stories that can cause pain. I have shared many stories about bravery, about being resilient and being afraid. While some may appear to have been similar, the experiences are never the same because they involve different times, different people and circumstances. One thing is for sure, I want to always cultivate a space where my students feel safe sharing their struggles and their successes. For me, it wasn't that long ago that my sister passed away. We taught at the same school and losing her was terribly painful, but I was very fortunate to have been able to work with an amazing group of staff members that looked after me during my difficult teaching moments.

I get to use my classroom as a platform for collaboration with brilliant minds. I am in charge of developing meaningful lessons that will challenge my students and broaden their awareness for life. In my classroom, I get to be the warden of service and work with the future leaders that can also follow the footsteps of amazing leaders like Elon Musk, Martin Luther King Jr., Mahatma Gandhi, Cesar Chavez, Albert Einstein, and many others who stood for world peace, creativity, inventions, and changing our world.

As I set out to continue walking a path of self-discovery and collaboration with leaders in order to awaken the giant in me, my heart is full. I stand proud because something I did with my students will manifest into something bigger than what you or I can ever imagine. I can't wait to see what my students from Suva Elementary will become and how their presence and role in the world will change the world for a better place to live!

Creating authentic moments of learning, paving the road to collaboration to where students create moments of meaningful experiences, is what I wish for. I work diligently to support students taking charge of their learning, which can lead to great benefits. This is what I like to call a win-win strategy. Students feel important and valued not just by teachers but by their peers. Teachers see the fruits of their labor and those results can be extremely gratifying.

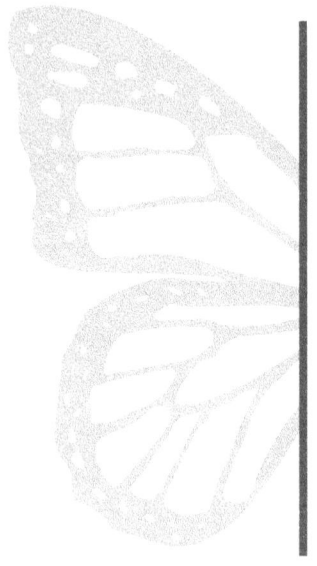

Chapter Six

Working through the Struggles

CHAPTER SIX: WORKING THROUGH THE STRUGGLES

As teachers, sometimes we encounter challenges that may limit our ability to perform and produce extraordinary results. There can be times when our strength is lacking force and the need to be elsewhere is the only thing that can bring us comfort. I witnessed such an event in my life. My sister, who used to teach with me, went on maternity leave, and while she was out on pregnancy leave, she encountered complications days after giving birth to a baby girl and she passed away. I felt like my teaching career was over and I could never return to what I loved doing, especially without my sister.

> "The Struggle You're in Today,
> Is Developing the Strength
> You Need for Tomorrow"
>
> —Robert Tew

It was a little over four months after my sister, Maribel, had passed away. My leave of absence from work would end, and I knew I would need to return to work. My mind was full of clutter and confusion, and I entertained the thought of not returning to work at all. I was sad and worried about having a breakdown at work. I was consumed with many mixed emotions. The voices in my head were loud; the questions came and went. As much as I had loved teaching, I actually started questioning my return and ability to perform. The story I kept telling myself was I couldn't go back to the same school my sister and I taught at for ten years. It would be too painful and awkward. I had imagined that perhaps a million questions would be addressed to me and I wouldn't be able to handle that.

Since childhood, my sister and I did many things together. We were inseparable. Teaching together was just another experience we shared together. She and I would carpool to and from work, have recess and lunch together, and plan for school together. Her classroom was right in front of mine. The first face to greet me when I would open the door for morning recess, lunch, and after school was hers. I could see her arm signaling me in sign language as she held up three fingers meaning we were leaving at three o'clock. Our school day began at 8:00 a.m. and ended at 2:00 p.m., so staying for one hour after class was usually the cut-off. My sister was always excited to get home to her son, Jacob, so being ready to leave school on time was very important even if it meant taking some work home.

Driving to and from work with my sister was always a blast. Sometimes we talked each other into taking a small detour and ended up at a nearby Target, Sprouts, or Michael's. I loved being a victim of her game and going on a last-minute impulse-buy shopping spree with her. She usually had to stop and buy the necessities for my nephew Jacob, and I would enjoy watching her face light up as she shopped for the love of her life. Pampers, wipes, an outfit or two, and of course a book to go along with the items.

Our conversations on the way home filled the car with stories of our passions and love for teaching. I admired the love my sister had for her students and how she went above and beyond for them. She had a special way of connecting with them and had unique ways of showing she cared. She loved being invited to attend little league games for her students.

One day we went shopping and she purchased a pair of shoes that looked too small for her size and much too big for her son. She was shopping for a student whose family was less privileged, and

CHAPTER SIX: WORKING THROUGH THE STRUGGLES

her student was in desperate need of shoes. My younger sister was loving, compassionate, and loyal to her students. I looked up to her and often told her how proud of her I was. She was an amazing mother, daughter, wife, and teacher. She was my guide even though she was one year younger than me. I always learned so much from her. Many were fond of her, and she was respected by many who were privileged to know her.

Maribel's smile was infectious, her smile could light up the room. Her witty ways would spark a chuckle here and there. The rigor and respect she radiated in the classroom was admirable and I valued learning from her work ethic and habits. My sister would often say, "When you work in something you love, it's not really work." Although I heard these words very frequently, I never knew how much those words would mean to me like they do now that she is gone.

My sister loved being a teacher, and one thing that made my career special was sharing the experience with her. I treasured the almost ten years of collaborating together, planning together, laughing together, driving to work and back together, and stopping off at my parents' house for dinner after our Wednesday meetings. Those were the few things we enjoyed doing, and I really missed that. I long to have those moments again.

The morning drive to work the day of my return in my silver Infiniti G35 was quiet. All I could hear was the sound of my car's motor and the street noise of the cars that drove past me. I took my time to get to work that morning, and I could see almost every car drive past me, but I was in a daze. I looked down into my coffee holder, and there was only one cup of coffee: mine. The smell was faint; my cup of coffee didn't produce the same aroma that two cups of coffee do, especially in a car. The speakers in my car were used to playing Mariachi music, The Cranberries, Bon Jovi, or R&B

"feel good" music. The only sound in my car that morning was my voice. I spoke to her as if she were sitting in the passenger seat, and told her it would be weird returning to work without her. I told her I would miss seeing her face as I opened my classroom door and looked over toward her classroom. I wondered who would be there in her place.

As I pulled into our school parking lot, I glanced over to what used to be her favorite parking spot. It was as if someone knew not to park there because they knew she could be driving up soon. I parked my car there, and just as I parked, there was a knock on my window. One of the teachers at my school was waiting for my arrival. I was greeted with a huge smile and an enormous hug. "Welcome back, Ms. Ramos!" I was overwhelmed by the welcome I received that morning.

As I made my way down the hall toward the front office, I was stopped a few times by teachers who welcomed me and offered their support. I felt the warmth, compassion, and heartfelt love from my colleagues. I knew I would be fine and that I would be able to continue with my teaching journey even if my sister would not be there to share our school's triumphs with me. The celebrations would not be the same, but they were one thing I would hold true to. Teaching with all my heart and being true to what I once called my love, before my sister passed away, still had some of my attention, and I desired to continue on what could be an amazing path.

Teaching was a way for me to do what I loved doing and push myself to work outside of my comfort zone. Returning to work without my sister and still being in the same school was definitely outside my comfort zone. But teaching through the struggles may have large rewards.

My sister's absence was something that I struggled with. I needed to change the perspective I had on coming out of a loved one's death. I was willing to receive and let in all the good light that my colleagues would shine upon me as they welcomed me back to school. I was back and I would hold my sister's spirit inside my heart and teach with all of mine. No struggle is too big when you have your heart in it.

That experience taught me to be tenacious and push through the struggles I encountered no matter what. I went back to work and my words were short and I experienced many silent moments. My heart ached; my mind often had chatter and wandering thoughts. I longed to see her smile one more time as I opened my classroom door. I wanted our eyes to meet again and I wanted to gaze over to her side of the hallway and see her look at her students as they entered her classroom and how she greeted some with her beautiful smile. My sister had infectious enthusiasm and energy, but this time only the angels in heaven would be greeted by her.

Her death tested me in many ways, and to date it has been the most excruciating emotional pain I have had to endure. While I was faced with many uncertainties and often questioned numerous things, I knew I could count on the great teaching staff at my school. Our school is known for one thing: people always say Suva Elementary staff is the friendliest and most supportive. I now say that myself.

Life after death is different for everyone. The memories people leave us with are very overwhelming and I found myself drowning in vast emotions from time to time, especially at school, on my way home. Sometimes I would drive to the cemetery and just sit at her grave and talk to her about my day at work. Sometimes I would tell my sister about her former students and their families coming to me to see how our family was doing after her death.

While sometimes I hoped for something that would never happen, my dream to fulfill what my sister and I set out to do was waiting. I just never imagined that I would start a business and continue teaching without her. Teaching at my school holds a lot of memories and beautiful sentiments about working with my sister and a void in the hearts of others who loved her.

My sister's death left a hole in my heart, and left an empty classroom for some time, but this experience also allowed me to understand the importance of my existence in a classroom—in a classroom where young minds are being shaped by thoughts and experiences worth sharing and creating better ones later. I have given myself permission to heal from this experience and grow from it. The struggles will always be there, but a teacher in constant movement toward leading with passion and love can overcome anything and can lead to having breakthroughs in education! What struggles have made you stronger and allowed you to become a better person?

While that dream has paved another road, I have taken a path where I am nurturing the idea of creating something bigger for teachers. I have come to the realization that my time has come. I will take a leap of faith, plunge into a world where I get to explore being a content creator for teachers. My plan is to design a program for teachers where social-emotional learning and having a growth mindset meet. I know this book is only the beginning and as I write the words on this page, I hope to pave an idea that will lead to a road with beautiful experiences, which will spark an interest for those looking into pursuing a career in education to stay, for those who stand for enriching the lives of students and being the beacon of love, guidance, support and building strong relationships with students.

After my sister's death, I reminded myself and my students that we can all make a difference—but the question to think about is, *What kind of difference do we want to make? How will our actions support others?*

CHAPTER SIX: WORKING THROUGH THE STRUGGLES

My return to work wasn't always an easy hurdle to cross. I am grateful for the friendships and new relationships I made along the way. They are relationships that matter and are worth talking about. Because of my love for teaching, I have spent the last ten years learning from leaders that have inspired me to pursue my dreams and make time for me to work on myself. In order for me to provide my best service to my students, I need to stay mentally healthy. My mentors have guided me to think about what I have done in my profession to inspire others, create a positive change and instill an awareness in my students to understand how to take care of their bodies and deal with challenging times at home and school. Together we can all overcome the struggles that we face, but we must remember to commit to what matters the most and why it is important! These are all important things to reflect upon because it is part of the core of teaching.

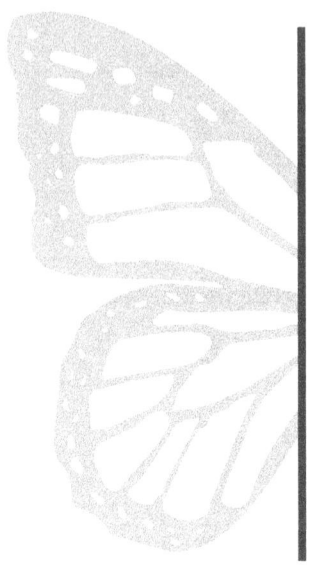

Chapter Seven

Courage to Write

CHAPTER SEVEN: COURAGE TO WRITE

One morning on my way to work, I decided to do something I normally don't do on my drive into school. I had been listening to a podcast on meditation a few days before and decided that morning to give myself the gift of silence. Those who know me know that I am quite a chatterbox and enjoy the company of others and welcome conversation more frequently than not.

That day I decided I would change my morning routine. As I walked out my front door, I stopped to observe the plants in my front yard, tugged on the leaves of the tree in front of me, and then proceeded to get into my car. The minute I turned on the car, the morning talk radio show was playing music. I quickly reached for the radio dial and turned it off. The usual call I make to my mother driving to work would not happen that day.

I drove down the street and noticed my neighbors walking their two dogs. I approached the crosswalk and noticed the mist falling and landing gently on the hood of the cars that were parked on the street. The neighbors' lawns were wet from the fog that had settled during the course of the night and earlier that morning. It was a cold foggy drive to work that day.

It was such a wonderful opportunity for me to look at life on the fifteen-minute drive to work through a different lens. I saw pedestrians walking without a care, the train that usually held up traffic for at least six or seven minutes sped through the tracks with tons of cargo to transport to another location. The famous Broguiere's Dairy in Montebello on Maple Avenue had the usual regular customers ready to purchase their favorites from this local historic dairy. Some students were waiting to cross the street to one of Montebello

Unified School District's newest Pathways High School, ATC. As I proceeded through the intersection, I wondered how many of my former students were attending that high school. My short drive was coming to an end (I only work about five miles from home). I continued to be mesmerized by the scene outside my window, the sounds of cars and trucks driving past me, the honking of other drivers to warn others about a vehicle stalled on the right lane while other drivers kindly gave others the right of way. I acknowledged a friendly wave from another driver as he thanked me for allowing him to have the right of way; after all, I had plenty of time to get to school that day.

As I approached Suva Street that morning, I wondered if the security guard that usually patrols the factory on the corner of our street was actually happy working there. I wondered how early the workers at another company actually began their shift, because at about 7:30 a.m. some were already outside having breakfast at the lunch truck parked in the parking lot. I wondered some more and drove the extra five hundred feet before I pulled and made a left turn into the school parking lot.

I walked to my classroom, and before I actually opened the door, I started thinking about how my students are the future and I have a lot to learn from them. My commitment as their teacher is huge. I know my students will venture into the world in a few years and some will probably find a cure for illnesses, some may invent something amazing to protect our world, and some may just *be* and *do* whatever their heart desires. Some students will probably wonder about wandering. I wondered if they would actually still remember me.

I reached for the lanyard that usually hangs around my neck and grabbed the key. I opened the door, looked around the room before I turned on the lights, and set up my computer for the day.

CHAPTER SEVEN: COURAGE TO WRITE

Like Tony Robbins says, in many of his workshops, I was priming for my work-day, and one thing I started doing that I learned at a personal development workshop was to find a mindful moment to meditate and set my intention for the day. Prime time was part of my daily routine, and that day it would be done differently. I had a job that granted me satisfaction and joy, and I was surrounded by wonderful opportunities to grow. Maybe it wasn't the best-paying job, but it truly was a noble and rewarding profession.

My drive to work that morning was not only to observe the world around me but also to think about my story—the story I have always wanted to share and write about my life as a teacher. This new writing journey is possible because my students' words drive me to pursue a dream that could create inspiration or value for others. Perhaps my story could be another platform used to inform others about the joy that the teaching profession can bring into your life if you allow it to and how students' inspiration can drive you to be an extraordinary teacher.

My story would be the first of many ideas I actually put into writing, and the main character was me. Through my story, readers would discover my feelings, my fears, my struggles, my triumphs, my disappointments, and my personal inspiration for continuing to teach, be bold in my profession, and thrive to be better every time I step in front of a classroom.

I committed to finding a mentor that would guide me on my writing journey. I knew that by committing to this dream I would be exposing myself to many who would read my book. I was willing to let you, and others, know about my personal story and what brought me immense satisfaction as a teacher. In my opinion, it takes a warrior to teach elementary school kids.

As the day began, all I thought about was my drive to work that day and how I was able to notice my surroundings and capture the spirit of life, see how the same strangers share my morning commute just from a distance.

I was looking forward to sharing the news with my students and how our writing time after recess would have stellar stories with vivid characters, enticing details, and the best endings of an eight-year-old writer. I could use the experiences I had with my students to support me with my plan; daily writing and planning would be constant practice both at school and home.

I felt a sense of urgency to get home that day so I could write in my journal and begin a new vision board with all the details that would be the next big goal for me.

I would investigate the process of writing a book, complete it, and publish it. I gave myself permission to write about my teaching journey as an elementary school teacher. I discovered that for many years I entertained the idea of letting fear take over my passion and keep me from accomplishing one more thing on my personal bucket list. For a long time I gave my fears permission to stay close by and keep me occupied with all of my attention on thinking: what if my book isn't good enough, what if it doesn't resonate with others, how long should it be? Will the book be what others need? What if people criticize it? What if it fails? I allowed the chatter in my head—some of us call it the committee—to overpower my thinking and allowed the fear to grow. What if it failed?

I knew that if I wanted to pursue my dream as an author, my mindset had to change. I could either choose to think vaguely about the book idea or change my vision for why I was writing and allow my heart to speak to you. I thought two years into the future and could see myself at book signings, conferences, and speaking engagements. I knew I still wanted to serve people and continue teaching but through a different avenue. What good is a Ferrari if you don't drive it and leave it parked in the garage? You leave it parked and it begins to get dirty from the dust that settles over time in your garage. The Ferrari is a fine vehicle, shiny and fast, ready to be taken for an amazing ride on the road. When you think about why it is parked in the garage, you answer your own question: I don't want anything to happen to it. I don't want it to get dirty or mess it up. I'm scared . . . it's an expensive car. Guess what? Life is meant to be lived, and so the Ferrari is meant to be driven. It's like the slogan BMW had for a while, "It's the ultimate driving machine." When you get the courage to drive the car, you'll be amazed at what you feel and how many heads will turn when they see the beautiful car and hear the sounds of the motor drive past them.

My writing is the same idea. When I mustered up the courage to write, I felt a sense of ease and relief. I found myself feeling very overwhelmed because there was so much I wanted to say about my experience, my time in education, and the love I have felt from and for my students and peers. I came to the realization that it wasn't about how I would tell you about my experiences or the struggles I have experienced throughout my career that made me want to stay in teaching; these experiences touched me in such a way that my heart was full of gratitude and admiration for every student that embraced their learning opportunity and made huge efforts to persevere with determination. I know, you're probably wondering how this could be, since studies show most teachers walk away from teaching because of the demands that go along with the job, reaching a burn-out period before completing their fifth year. I often wonder what those people are doing instead and wonder if they are truly working in a profession that brings them joy. Having a job that brings you joy is fulfilling.

Well, one teacher (ME) working for the Montebello Unified School District at Suva Elementary feels differently. Trust me, teaching could be your next best job, but you need to understand that only the bravest stick it out. Only the strongest survive. Only the most passionate and daring individuals are truly the ones who make a huge difference in the lives of students and in the teaching profession. The teachers who allow themselves to be seen in their most humble and vulnerable state, those who open up their hearts and allow themselves to be loved, are the purest form of being what some may call "the core teacher."

I have reached a place in my career where I am challenging myself to show up in the teaching space differently. I stand for educators, for those who want to pursue a career in the field of teaching and for those who dream of being better than their own teachers. I hold teachers on a pedestal. We are the ones who ignite the flame of learning, the ones who encourage the young leaders to pursue their dreams, the ones who motivate our students to continue growing and captivate them with our abilities to create the most extraordinary learning opportunities for them. Every time I pushed myself to grow, my students were able to benefit from my effort. I felt an overwhelming feeling of gratitude and joy because I knew I was the source that molded them to question "why?" and "how?" during their learning process and truly develop a huge love for learning.

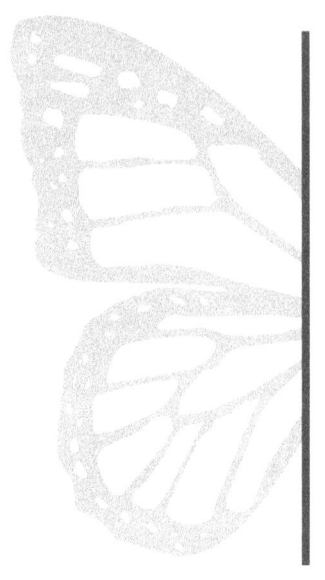

Chapter Eight

My Fourth-Grade Teacher, Mr. Anderson

CHAPTER EIGHT: MY FOURTH-GRADE TEACHER, MR. ANDERSON

They say inspiration comes not only from experiences but also from people who have touched our lives in such a way that we feel a unique connection with them. Sometimes our world shifts and we end up getting so wrapped up in our own interpretations and experiences that we neglect to think about events that caused changes in our childhood. Childhood moments can stay dormant for a long time, and, when we face another reality later in life, we are taken back to a different time where perhaps certain events trigger new ideas or feelings in the present. Sometimes we may face the unimaginable and may not realize that certain people in our lives were significant. As a teacher, I have been able to work through various ways where I have been able to return to my past and be in a time where teachers were the cause for me feeling an overwhelming sense of gratitude and appreciation. I don't know if they will ever know how much they mattered.

I grew up in a community where kids had opportunities to play together on the city street without worrying about being exposed to negativity or hostile environments. Kids often came over to my house to play, and my friends' mothers stayed a while and spent their afternoon talking about random things and watching us all playing without a care in the world. Our time there was short, but the memories created living there left an everlasting impression in my mind and heart. Besides the pure innocence of childhood and friends racing around the block, riding bicycles at the city park, and walking to our local library, some of my best moments there were made possible by teachers who cared and believed in their students, including me. Perhaps some of these teachers may not remember me, but one thing is for sure, I remember them and how they made me feel. Waking up Monday through Friday was a treat for me. I couldn't wait for morning to come and get ready for school. I loved being a student at Rosewood Park Elementary, and to this day I can remember the names of all of my teachers and many of my experiences there. The relationships and friendships I had as a student there were very special, and I still keep in touch with some of my childhood friends.

Relationships should never be taken for granted. Instead, they should be nurtured, treated with care, and revisited so they can remain strong and pure. The relationships I made with my teachers in my elementary school were a long time ago, but some remain in my mind and are dear to me.

Rosewood Park Elementary was walking distance from my home and I could see it when I stood in my front yard. I remember many of the events held at my school, the teachers who taught there, walking to the city library once a week with my third-grade class and seeing my grandma or aunt standing outside my front yard and waving to me as I walked by. I remember my fourth-grade teacher, Mr. Anderson. He had a silly way of calling me by my full name, Leticia, which I disliked until I was about thirty-something years old. He was a short man with sandy-brown hair and a funny little mustache. He always wore corduroy pants with the perfect crease down the middle, and always looked sharp and ready to start his teaching day.

I enjoyed being in fourth grade and having Mr. Anderson as my guide. He was someone to laugh with, who motivated us all to do better, and I enjoyed his way of making us understand that developing a strong sense of identity and caring about our education was the key to excelling in school. He promoted self-accountability. He had a unique style about teaching and he would make us care

CHAPTER EIGHT: MY FOURTH-GRADE TEACHER, MR. ANDERSON

about our future and making every second count. Perhaps it was his unusual ways of teaching and how he cultivated our learning environment and the relationships formed inside our classroom. Mr. Anderson would make time to "talk" to us about his interests, his family, and his thoughts about school and post-secondary education. Many times, I wished my father and I could have those conversations at home.

I remember circle time and how he would captivate all of us with his ability to read stories by Judy Blume. He brought *Tales of a Fourth Grade Nothing* to life. He could transform himself into all the characters and make funny voices for certain characters in the story. It's like he was another Robin Williams. We laughed a lot in that class. We would make time to have authentic conversations about what we were reading and why it mattered. I never really said much; I mostly listened and was reluctant to speak because I had a heavy Spanish accent and, to some extent, felt a bit of shame because of it. I had challenges keeping up with the rest of the class and making sense of what I read. Comprehension was hard for me, and I often ran from it. Although I could read fluently, recalling information was sometimes a difficult task to overcome. Mr. Anderson allowed me to see that my challenges with reading were just different ways for me to learn about what I was reading. Sitting in the back of the room for reading time was where most of my learning happened. "Just read," he would say, "and you'll discover the magic in the story."

Mr. Anderson's fourth-grade class was special because we had pets in our classroom. I remember our class pet, the salamander, whose habitat was a glass fish tank that sat on the old beat-up wooden cabinet by the window near the back door. We had mice for feeding the classroom snake. I couldn't believe what our classroom snake could do when it was time for another meal. Now that I think about it, Mr. Anderson was pretty rad. My dad had a rule: absolutely no pets in our home. At least I had the experience of owning one from Monday through Friday in class because Mr. Anderson made that experience possible. Steven Anderson was the source of making many possibilities available for a nine-year-old girl who feared to speak up because English was her second language, who struggled in school because her parents hardly spoke English, who always wanted to have a pet but her dad refused, who had a hard time understanding what she read because paying attention to details in a story was challenging.

I am very fortunate to have had such an extraordinary teacher. It was odd—I didn't have a close relationship with my dad, but my fourth-grade teacher was my role model and I felt closer to him than my dad. I felt safe in his class. My father would always tell me to respect my teachers and to learn as much as I could from them. I spoke to my father about Mr. Anderson from time to time, and he always appreciated that I could have a great person to guide me through the important details in life.

Our class was often reminded that we were leaders and encouraged to contribute our ideas and expertise in order to spruce up our learning time. Together, we formed opinions and had conversations that would often lead to open discussions about other interesting topics. Mr. Anderson had the amazing ability to make us appreciate our learning process. He encouraged us to embrace the struggles and would take no excuses from his students. This man had a very unique way of helping us stay focused, and he held us all accountable for our personal academic growth.

Being a fourth grader made me feel important and I had a sense of belonging. I longed to be with my friends, who at the time were like a family. I owe those feelings of gratitude and being successful to Mr. Anderson. He created a nurturing environment for all, he made us understand that education was the common denominator for creating an experience that gave us opportunities to challenge ourselves to be better, that it was important for promoting growth and the key to advancing in the world. How would you feel if students expressed their gratitude and took time to reflect about their childhood education and you were the teacher that made a difference for them?

Due to the negativity that can evolve in our education system and in our own schools, I wish more teachers took the time to nurture the relationships they have with their students. If only they had the energy and courage to help students learn through their struggles and failures and remind them that being successful isn't always an easy task. Building strong relationships and creating different ways to reach a child is important, but most importantly, keeping the desire and passion to teach even while facing struggles can lead to remarkable benefits, for both teachers and students. The bigger the struggle, the bigger the gain!

Thank you, Steven Anderson for making me smile, allowing me to see that taking a risk can lead to great results and fear is just another variable in the equation—with a solution!

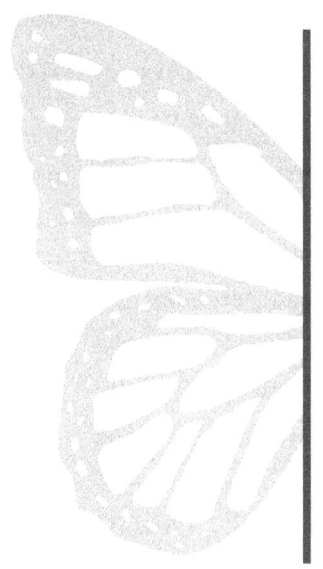

Chapter Nine

Leaving Our Legacy

CHAPTER NINE: LEAVING OUR LEGACY

One day I was sitting in my home office browsing through the internet for ideas to decorate my classroom on everyone's favorite website: Pinterest. I have to admit, if I am not careful, I find myself spending more time than I should browsing through the website. Pinterest is great for many things and can be extremely useful and a lifesaver especially if you are a teacher looking for inspiration for your classroom or new ideas that lead to having well-thought-out lessons.

That particular day, I stumbled on a quote by the famous Mahatma Gandhi: "Be the Change You Wish to See in the World." I stared at the words on the page. The words were few, but they captivated me and held such an important message. I felt a strong urge to investigate more quotes by leaders like Gandhi, leaders who made a difference and left a legacy for us to learn from and aspire to be like.

As an elementary school teacher, I often wonder about other teachers who have created a movement in education and stood up for something bigger and better, who were respected by many. My curious nature is in constant thought about the passions that drove them to make changes that left a legacy that motivates and inspires others to follow their path.

A few years ago, I was mentored by a professor who asked our mastermind group to describe what our life as educators could be like if we shifted the way we think about our careers. I thought about what I could do as a teacher to be the change in education. He asked us to think about the great things we were already doing and to increase our level of commitment so that we could produce bigger gains. I questioned my ways of delivering lessons and the types of conversations I wanted to have every day with my students. I knew my professor's purpose for holding the class in that manner was important and his intention for running his class that way would eventually allow all of us to have our breakthroughs, but first we all had to do the work to see our gains. I needed to evaluate myself and my educational goals so I could have a new commitment.

Back then, things didn't resonate with me the way they do today. I give credit to the personal growth workshops and training I have since taken. These experiential training courses have allowed me to work on being present with myself, focusing on things I can control and deciding how I choose to feel about things that occur in my life. In these sessions I have learned to think at a higher level of consciousness. I wish I had taken those workshops earlier in my career because they have helped me learn tremendously about myself, my life, and my professional career. While the work on myself is a continuous journey and requires commitment, I am willing to continue because I know it's an extra dose of constant evolution into a better human and having an amazing quality of life. I have been able to understand why I need to make every moment count in my life and in my job. Making life intentional is essential and doing the same inside a classroom is also important. Being able to hold the power to have a conversation that matters and is worth sharing is key to having remarkable results and can lead to higher levels of student success.

As teachers, it is important to take caution on what we do and how we do things in school. It's extremely vital that we slow down and tune in to what our students are really saying. Are we really listening to what students are saying? Students are like characters in a story; their roles must be fulfilled in order for them to feel successful in their setting (the classroom). I have found that it is important to be able to read our students like a book and note the important details about them. What do they mean when they speak? Sometimes students don't verbally say anything to us, but their actions do all the talking. I know our work can be challenging and paying attention to certain mannerisms is also more work for us, but it is a necessary task if we want to be great at what we do.

Reading our students carefully and being intentional about why we spend the time we do with them is important. I came to the realization that as a teacher I really needed to pay attention to their needs. Every student articulates messages in their own unique way and sometimes their message is misunderstood. I often questioned what my students were trying to tell me when they were late, when they turned in messy homework , when they were picked up over an hour late, or when they were falling asleep in class. With the correct tools, an effective teacher can skillfully know what their students need and be a part of the solution.

Changes can appear without notice in our learning environment and we are often faced with the challenge to act upon each unique event effectively. Aside from our daily job assignments, we are constantly obligated to attend meetings after school or workshops outside of board day. Even so, some teachers just get the job done; they are content and try to stay positive. These teachers are sometimes ridiculed and even criticized for that. These teachers are the game-changers! They make the impossible possible and get the tasks at hand done with little or no training.

I have heard of teachers just watching their life pass before them, sitting on the sidelines and criticizing other teachers who go above and beyond for their students. They criticize the teachers who make extra time to provide support for their students, and sometimes they fail to commit to their teaching responsibilities enthusiastically and in a professional manner. Look, if you want to talk about other teachers who are performing better than you, or standing out at your school, then maybe it's because you want something they have. If your focus is on pointing out what others are doing, it's because there is something about those teachers you wish you had or could do.

- What would it be like for you if you took a different approach to the judgments you make and looked for the good qualities in the teacher or teachers you are criticizing?
- How would your relationship with those teachers be?
- What could that teacher offer you? What could you learn from them?

My intent is simply to give you some points to think about and reflect on. Let me just tell you that if you felt a bit uncomfortable by the questions I posed, then you have something to ponder about. Whether you like it or not, it is a sign that something is puzzling you. Maybe it wasn't the words on this page; maybe it was the notion behind my questions—now I ask you to think about why you felt that way. Give yourself time to think about it without judgment and find the answer because it's in you! Sometimes what we need to focus our attention on is our mindset. We need to think about how we think and move toward a direction where positivity lies.

A quest for change in education has been an idea that has flourished in my mind and continues to be the essential drive for me promoting that anything is possible for my students. As a teacher, it has been my mission to instill the values that lead to having a positive mindset in order to seek better results in school. Not all students understand that mistakes are to be embraced and can actually make us better individuals. Students don't always understand that we are responsible for our actions and that creating new habits of positive change can lead to extraordinary results. They need to be taught that leaders can see challenges as new possibilities and growth!

One brave principal, Linda Cliatt-Wayman from Strawberry Mansion High School, stepped up to a vicious challenge and turned the school upside down. With the help of her staff and other members of the community, she worked diligently to create a major plan to convert the school and change the students' philosophy about their education. She was the champion that students needed. This story resonated with me because I understood that my students also needed me. Despite the issues we face in my classroom, students need a person who will love them and develop a relationship that matters. They need a teacher who can give authentic experiences for learning, take risks, and lead. I found it necessary to stay in teaching and be the best imaginable role model for them. When I see the crucial need to promote authentic learning experiences, the need to create a storm of beautiful ideas and human interaction, I find the urge to stay in teaching and be the best imaginable role model for my students.

Sometimes we show up to work and feel the need to be elsewhere or want to tend to our personal needs. Instead, we get into our well-known routine and create an amazing learning opportunity for our students. Principal Cliatt-Wayman spoke in a TED talk about the importance of making students feel important and leading without excuses. She was determined to set a new tone and expectations for students at Strawberry Mansion High School. She stated, "We can only see what they will become . . ." For Linda, making sure her students had a better understanding and cared about their education was important. Paving the way to intentional teaching and learning was important at the school. Not all are willing to go the extra mile like that. Teachers aren't always willing to go the extra mile for their students and sometimes are unaware of their expectations.

Trying to find a way so that all of my students feel important, capable, and respected is my focus. Working hard every day so that my students feel comfortable and safe enough to arrive at school every day is a daily routine. Every day I do what I can to make them want to stay and work like champions. Even during the bad times, sad times, frustrating times, and shitty days. Let's face it, we all have shitty days as teachers. When you show up at work and you are willing to put your negative emotions aside and focus on creating an amazing day for your students and yourself, you'll be surprised to know how much of an impact your students make on you. The love they feel for you and the admiration they have toward you is huge. After all, remember that to your students you are like their mother or father because many times your students cannot rely on their own parents due to exterior circumstances.

For some of us, our students are truly like our own kids. I've been a teacher for over twenty-two years; I do not have my own children, but my students have given me the opportunity to get a taste of what it could be like. Some of you reading this book right now probably have needed to help clothe some students, provide food for them, or drive them to certain places in order to meet a need or needs. You have gone to their little league or other sport games, have stayed after school to provide additional support for them, and have gone far beyond the school day for them and their family too.

So after your labor of love is done for the day or week, how do you truly feel? Okay, besides the typical answers we get—tired, drained, and ready for a drink, glad it's Friday. How does your heart feel knowing you showed up to work the way you did? How do you feel knowing your students got the best of you that day and you made someone smile? How do you feel knowing you made a difference that week? These are some of the things I love about my job.

CHAPTER NINE: LEAVING OUR LEGACY

It excites me to see that my young leaders act on caring about their education and work diligently to perform better. I welcome conversations that ignite the fire to set new goals and together establish things students need from me. I appreciate their beautiful smiles, sense of humor, and ideas every day. The relationships I have created with my students have given me many opportunities to be my whole self. I get to be who I love being and encourage them to do the same without fear. My students have given me strength and encouragement. They are so innocent and even think their teacher is the most amazing human being with superpowers. My students have been able to see my greatness when I couldn't. Sometimes it was my students who motivated me to do something new and think outside my box. It was my seven- and eight-year-old students who told me I had to recommit to my dream and chase it. "No dream is ever too big, Ms. Ramos," were words I often heard flowing through my classroom. They were repeating what I would often say, but I was guilty of not always putting my words into action.

> Thank you, students for seeing what
> I couldn't see sometimes.

> Thank you for being the light when times were dark.

> Thank you for inspiring me to live my
> dream and chase a bigger one.

Our students have the amazing ability to step out into the world and conquer great things. Some of our students will remember your words, remember how you made them feel, remember how you ran your classroom—and some will remember how much you valued them and cared.

If you want your students to show up and be heard, it is your job to craft the idea so that students get it and feel comfortable being fearless and proactive participants in your class. It is my job to tend to my students and motivate them to chase their dreams and seize the moments where learning is happening! This road may not be the easiest to stay on, but consistency, tenacity, and passion will be important to embrace while on this path. The legacy we leave can initiate a new beginning of another educational endeavor for a student who could one day leave a legacy for others to follow too.

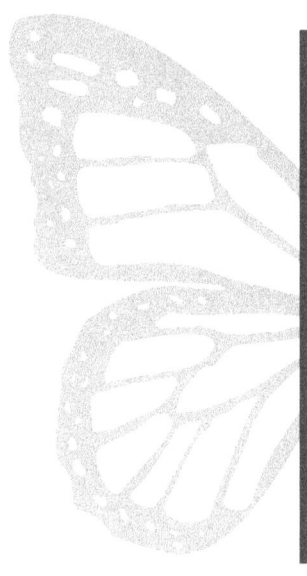

Chapter Ten

Inspiration

CHAPTER TEN: INSPIRATION

As the years pass and I stop to reflect about my profession, I can't imagine life without teachers. Teachers that truly have a heart, want to work with others, and make a difference. Teaching can be like feeding your soul—feeding your soul with the beautiful, insightful messages from our dear students. The students that one day will venture off into our world and become something bigger than they were when they crossed paths with you for the first time.

It saddens me to learn that there is a dark truth to the notion of more teachers turning away from teaching and leaving the profession for good. Teachers are reaching a burnout period and they can't handle the pressures that go along with this noble job. In my experience I think teachers aren't given enough opportunities to obtain tools that support in solving problems that are related to emotional stress. I have read numerous books on cognitive coaching and mindset practices for teachers that explain how to ease the stress and overload of emotions teachers may feel when the workload is high. That's why I always say, "Self love first." Taking care of oneself is key to having the energy and positive mindset to be an effective teacher and carry on with duties that are required to be successful in this career.

Oftentimes, I think about who may need my support and guidance the most. I ask myself, "How will the students benefit from what I have to say or how I simply show up in their space and teach?" The list goes on, many more questions cross my mind, and I will probably never know what all that entails, but one thing I know is that there is a teacher shortage and children need more individuals that will stay. The younger generation needs teachers that are on the forefront and advocating for them. Teachers that are sometimes willing to do the unimaginable and set goals that are almost irrational. Don't get me wrong when I say irrational, but sometimes it is important to set our bars high and work to accomplish tasks that really challenge us.

In Doctor Brené Brown's book, *Braving the Wilderness*, she mentions that experiences bring meaning. Teaching has been an amazing platform where I have been able to learn about many ideas, theories, and people and be part of a bigger and better story. It has been one of the most meaningful jobs I've had, one where I have needed to show up to work and be a certain way in order to be successful.

Teaching has been one of the highest summits I have reached. I have been challenged to work and be outside my comfort zone, I have taken new endeavors and created a learning space where my students feel comfortable leading lessons for others and feel safe in their learning community. For me, teaching is not only about content that promotes inquiry, it is a job that has given me the ability to teach my students not only about what the educational system says they need to know, but also about empathy, having compassion, being mindful about their environment and others, having the courage to take on challenges and exposing others to discover their greatness and use it. I am inspired by my students to continue sharing my love for being their teacher and together nurture the relationships we make.

Being Ms. Ramos has allowed me to be who I need to be for my students and bring an awareness to promoting an inclusive learning environment and promoting diverse cultures where all students feel welcomed and important. While this road was not always easy, it has given me an immense amount of satisfaction. Many times, I felt like I needed to lighten my load of teacher duties; let's face it, we all feel jaded and many times feel like taking a time out to chill and breathe. When I begin to feel the level of stress take over my body, I quickly shift my perception about the given idea and move toward what my wonderful thinkers, great problem solvers, compassionate friends, empathetic leaders, and daring students would benefit from and plan another course of action to take that could bring us all great pleasure and success.

One of the reasons I stayed in teaching was because I love being challenged to constantly evolve into a better person, or at least try to be. I have been able to learn things about myself and question if I could do better, could *be* better as a whole. I have been able to discover new passions and create new ways to evolve while introducing joy to stand out as my main feeling in my job.

Teachers, want-to-be teachers, and those who are thinking about joining others in the education field, please know that it takes time to adjust, but you matter and can make a terrific role model for our students. Teach because you will learn more about yourself than you'll ever know, you can change the level of consciousness and perception you currently have of yourself while teaching if you make the time to grow along the way. Grow by educating yourself on finding your own voice and allowing others to hear you, to know you, to want to follow you, and learn from you. Show up for work and make an everlasting impression on others so they will always remember you for being the voice of passion that was heard in the hallways, the phenomenal teacher who transcended their beauty through the love they radiated and respect you gave to others. Know that there are children in this world who are waiting for someone to be the change they need to see and be with to become inspired to flourish and produce exemplary results both in school and in their personal life. *You* are the capable one and the perfect one for many children and that is why I invite you to discover the wonderful qualities that this profession can give you. Teaching can be a very rewarding job.

Let your voice be heard, let your love shine through, and shake the world by being seen. Live your biggest dream early in your career. Let others know what you stand for and embrace every moment of your journey.

You can transmit life-long lessons and inspiring ideas to many people that come into your teaching circle. The lives of those who sit in my classroom and have been educated by me have been an important part of my life and have shown me amazing things about learning and developing new ways to love my job. Children have impacted my life in so many beautiful ways. They have truly been the strongest source for me when I needed someone to stand by my side and help me see the good during bad times. Being a teacher has definitely been an opportunity for me to grow along with, inspire, and love children. *You* can be the reason why someone has an extraordinary education, makes our world a better place, and becomes legendary!

In the past, I was blinded by my excuses, but now I am on a new road of discovery, inspiration, and change. I was chasing security instead of freedom and love! I was never envious of what others had but I entertained the thought about embracing another path where I could share my passion and embrace new opportunities to grow and create a shift in education.

One day, while researching, I came across Dr. Brené Brown's book, "The Gifts of Imperfection." Something drew me to learn more about her message. My feelings of learning intensified, I wanted to learn more about Dr. Brown, learn about her theories. Before I knew it, I was hooked and bought her books, read them and started taking notes on the ideas that resonated with me. It was clear to me. My failures, triumphs, frustrations, and gains were all part of my story and it was okay. Everything that happened to me during my teaching career was imperfectly perfect. My job and everything that came with it were all packaged perfectly; I was the protagonist in this story and couldn't hide it. I knew I had an opportunity to tell my story and hopefully others would understand that teaching can be amazing and worth every effort. Our world needs more teachers that will stay and create amazing experiences for students. Our students need teachers that will take a stand for educational justice, lead, love, believe that all students will make a difference, teach to the "core," and look past excuses for being great, greater or the greatest! Our students need teachers that will share their passion with the world and be educational leaders that will create inspiration one student at a time!

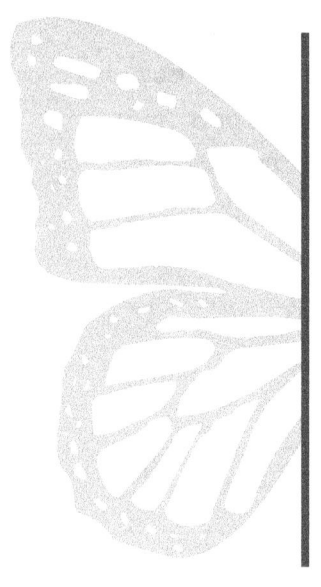

Chapter Eleven

Mr. "O"

CHAPTER ELEVEN: MR. "O"

One afternoon while sitting at my desk filling out papers, my eyes glanced upon this question: Name a teacher who has been an inspiration to you. I was taken back to a time when I was a sophomore in high school. Mr. Julian Olague was the name that stood out for me. I was privileged to have him as my softball coach, as well as my math teacher. Hearing his words of encouragement empowered me. For me, being at school was my preference. Life at home was not always a garden full of beautifully scented roses. Oftentimes, the smell of my home was faint and needed some watering of love and patience. On the field, I felt free to do what I loved, and it was a place where I laughed, played, and was surrounded by friends and mischief.

"Go out there and make a difference, do something big," were the words my teacher and softball coach used to say to us. Perhaps at the time those were just words passing through; things were not always easy in high school, and my home life wasn't exactly perfect. It amazes me how my coach's words resonate with me today as a teacher, and I find myself using those words with my students frequently. My students motivate me to make their life better, to wake up and be the best teacher that I can possibly be. All children deserve to be given the best education and feel amazed by the education they are receiving. Students should want to go to school and gain wonderful nuggets of wisdom. It is my job to spark an interest in our future inventors, creators, and explorers. Students should believe that they will discover a new quest for greatness and strength. This is how my coaches and their words made me feel.

One day I was in math class, and I vividly remember hearing my name called out. As I walked to the front of the classroom to get my test results from my coach and teacher, I felt a bit of discomfort and nervousness. "Thanks, Mr. O." I looked down at my paper and felt a sense of relief. Math wasn't my favorite subject, and I got a 76 percent, which was a "C"—a passing grade. As soon as the last person sat down, Mr. Olague walked to the front of the classroom and sat on the edge of his desk and looked at all of us. He had a stern look on his face, and it wasn't the same stern look I was used to getting on the softball field. There he was, our classroom giant, my mentor, my softball coach, influencer, and friend. I couldn't see his dimples that shone when he praised us and showed enthusiasm with us. He shook his head as his eyes were fixed on the ground. I felt nervous, my heart was beating fast and things felt awkward.

Then he began, "I want you all to take a look around this room, and I need you all to learn the faces of everybody in this room. Someday you will go on and make a huge difference in this world. People will know you and hopefully one day want to be inspired by you." Things were definitely getting weird because I had never heard Mr. O speak like that. Hearing his words of encouragement on the field was different than inside a classroom full of students who perhaps lacked enthusiasm and even struggled with math like me.

He further stated, "Latinos are always depicted as not being good enough . . . we tend to be last . . . according to society we are labeled as second-class citizens! I want you to care about your learning and know that I care very much about what I do and all of you." I grew up in a community with a mixed race of people. I glanced around the room and could see everyone listening attentively to his words and the uninterrupted silence had all of our attention. Mr. O's serious face looked different than it did on the softball field and sounded a bit sad.

CHAPTER ELEVEN: MR. "O"

The conversation unraveled into his childhood and his struggles to get to where he was today. Mr. Olague never opened up his math book that day. Our class may have not received a math lecture that day, but the lessons we did get were so much more than what a fifty-minute lesson could show me about algebraic equations. The chat with my teacher was priceless. He wanted to build our confidence and teach us to have the desire to improve our grades and to be willing to speak in class about our challenges in math. I was willing to make learning a priority in his class and change my attitude about how I saw math.

Algebra class was never the same. He lectured us on how we needed to give ourselves a vote of confidence to reach for the greater things in life. Conversations like the ones I had with my teacher are similar to the ones I have with my students. I muster up the will to keep them entertained with the idea that school is a great place for cultivating their dreams and a starting point where transcending dreams into a reality shape their future. School can be a place where greatness and changes build their future and where leaders flourish one student at a time.

Today Mr. Olague's message is clear, and I often find myself passing on the same message to my students and friends. I remind them about the importance of caring about their education, being ready to fuel up with new information to embrace the challenges and cultivate greatness within themselves. Mr. Olague's words of encouragement are a reminder that our words have power. As teachers, the messages we convey are to be expressed with caution. Our words can have so much value and meaning. I am frequently reminded of that conversation in math class and I reflect on Mr. Olague's message.

Staying in this profession as long as I have has been another way for me to see the world through the eyes of my students. When

I begin to think again and again about the core of my being, I realize that my previous teachers made a huge contribution to me being the teacher I am today. Today, I stand before my students in gratitude for allowing me to support every one of them in their educational quest for learning. I admire their courage, dedication, and efforts. I can only hope my students are able to share with others what they learned in my class, chase their dreams, and live the life they truly want to. I hope their future is bright and that they fuel their passion for growth with love and take on the world with confidence.

My curious mind continues to wonder about what they will think, feel, and say when asked what it meant to be a student learning inside room 20. I wonder how many of my students will write their story, share their story, and create amazing opportunities for us to learn from. One thing is for certain, many times in my career I discovered that the students I tried to inspire actually ended up inspiring me. These moments also fueled my decision to stay in teaching!

I appreciate the mentors I have had. I'm proud of myself for completing personal development training because I understand that my biggest gains were outside my comfort zone and being a leader means I need to be in constant growth. I wish more educators would give themselves this opportunity or be able to embark on these journeys because they are extremely beneficial.

If more teachers worked so that they can create a vision that holds their highest expectations, how would the teaching profession be? What if we all embarked on a journey of discovery, leadership, and building strong relationships with one another? What could we become as teachers if we went against some of the norms of what our educational system says we have to do and instead followed our heart and wrote our own curriculum?

CHAPTER ELEVEN: MR. "O"

For me, my profession has allowed me to feel like I transformed myself into a better individual.

Teaching has been like taking life-significant steps toward something better, building meaningful relationships, being led with love by my students, and supporting students one day at a time. My job has given me the opportunity to make decisions that allow me to use my time to be of service and support others. I have been able to be radical by creating things that were not going to happen otherwise and making bigger moments of change happen both for me and my students.

As teachers, we serve every day just by showing up and giving our time and energy to others. It's vital that teachers, or those looking to seek a profession in teaching, make time to cultivate moments of frequent collaboration where inquiry and ongoing discovery and creation are supported. As I think about how my previous teachers and students have inspired me in my teaching career, I realize that in some way they heard my messages, they understood what I was trying to say when we had chats in our classroom. They figured out how to reach me, say the right words, and be at the right place at the right time in order for me to be captivated by them. I often tell myself, "Be the teacher you want your child to have . . ." this is a motto I hold myself to and some of my friends use it too. If it's going to happen and I truly want to nurture that idea, it's important that I hold myself accountable to that every day; even when things get hectic and the morale may feel low.

Although I don't know this phenomenal woman personally, I feel this immense connection with Oprah Winfrey. Sometimes I wonder what she is doing at a given moment. I wonder what her thoughts are, I wonder what seeds she is planting. I think about what her grandest wishes are for this year. I know this may sound awkward, but her stories and contributions have moved me and make me want to learn more about her. Oprah's resilience and tenacious attitude are remarkable; she moves me and inspires me to be greater. This is a true example of how we can all make the world better when we give others our best and do it authentically by being transparent in who we are. Our light can shine upon others as they receive our best light and messages with love.

Sometimes I don't know if the choice I made is the right one; nevertheless, I aim to move one step closer to a new perspective and see the greatness around me. Oprah Winfrey has produced a great deal of content that I value immensely. She is a great example of strength and perseverance and I have been learning many things from her. As a teacher, something I value that Oprah speaks about is service. My profession has allowed me to provide the best educational experience to my students, I teach them to be strong-willed, to be compassionate toward others, to strive to be better friends and to have a positive mindset while working on their goals. I have been in service to other kids and in some cases adults too. When I am using my knowledge to teach and allow others to teach me, I am reminded that I hold the key to unlocking the world, my world, and moving into a direction of freedom that is manifested in many ways. I get to see new academic results in my students and embrace the experiences that we created in room 20.

I will continue to work daily to improve my teaching experiences and practices and that may look different than being inside a classroom. Sometimes I have needed to restructure my thoughts and figure out a way out of certain situations that don't settle with me because I am not always in agreement with our educational system and the norms I need to follow. Nevertheless, I strive to finish my day with grace and positivity, knowing I can always find a solution and there are more solutions than problems.

CHAPTER ELEVEN: MR. "O"

"Education is the key to unlocking the world, a passport to freedom."

—Oprah Winfrey

I went into this field intentionally. Teachers are overworked and underpaid—everybody knows that. Our job is shaping minds, shaping students' lives, and doing what we can because we care. Most of us have stayed in this profession because we will rise to the challenges of a strong work ethic while innovating and pushing through the daily struggles. My message to you is simply this:

You have the power to change a student's life. You can motivate a student to proceed and go off to a higher ranking in education. People like you and me can inspire others to do greater things. Be the teacher you wish your child had! You see, the teaching profession needs more people who are willing to commit to nurturing the concept of evolving through learning, developing relationships that matter, feeding their minds with wisdom from gurus who do things better and have been successful at it.

It's also important to plant the ideas where teaching professionals have educational breakthroughs, see great gains in their career and stand with resiliency while they practice leading in any given time.

Teachers need to reach out to faculty to recharge their batteries and have time to learn from one another. Never assume you know it all! Education is infinite. Stand up for your dream and live it. Listen to your heart, write your own story, spread love along the way, and see what sparks you. Share your wisdom. Think about how your presence will make others feel and perhaps your story will be what fuels them to make amazing things happen.

The core of teaching is a special way of life where an individual is the key element in another student's life. A teacher's greatest contribution can be discovering a student's talent, helping them learn to love learning and embrace the challenges even when things get tough. Teaching to the "core" means teachers practice the role of having more than one job in the classroom, smile through the struggles, be the spark of inspiration for others, and leave an impact in the world.

Chapter Twelve

Cultivating Gratitude

CHAPTER TWELVE: CULTIVATING GRATITUDE

Today I want to express my gratitude toward people who have made an impact on my life, both personally and virtually. I say virtually because I have never met people like Jay Shetty, Brené Brown, Robert Kiyosaki, Dr. Wayne Dyer, Dr. Miguel Ruiz, and Oprah Winfrey. Some have crossed my path via audio and some have ridden with me in the car, spoken to me in my living room, and gone to the gym with me. Their words are inspiring; I was truly captivated by their messages and philosophies. I became their biggest student. I once heard Dr. Wayne Dyer read the following quote at a conference, "When the student is ready, the teacher will appear." I frequently revisit this Buddhist proverb and interpret it differently every time. As a teacher, I was an eager student ready to listen to what these leaders had to say. The messages were important to me because I put into practice what I learned from them inside my classroom and in my own life.

Over the last few years, I have wanted to create a shift in my career and in my personal life and to make an effort to collaborate with influencers that have already made a huge impact in the world. As a teacher in constant movement toward making gains in education and in the lives of my students, being around people who inspire me and who have made significant contributions in my field is important for me. Cultivating an idea where I not only learn from amazing people but also welcome new ways to plan for new educational endeavors is something I want to continue to embrace. Being in a space of learning from leaders in education and business who have already accomplished major things has left me with a tremendous amount of ideas and theories to put into practice. If you want to be a better teacher, it is important to start writing a different narrative and work with leaders who bring you a lifetime of opportunities to share your expertise with others. Work from a place where you stand out, where people see you with great admiration and appreciate your authentic ways, where you reveal your passion for teaching and cultivating success.

Who have you been inspired by? What was that moment like? How would you describe the moment you knew you were hooked? When was the last time powerful leaders drew you in and captured your fullest attention? Where were you and what were you feeling at that moment? If you could look through that lens of self-reflection and consider what role models could capture your spirit and uplift you with their messages, who do you aspire to be like? Who do you see being the person for you to follow? Why?

When I stop and see where this notion is born, I trace it back to my years in elementary and high school. My teachers were my role models, they were the people I connected with and spent most of my years with besides my parents. The relationships I developed with them meant so much and still do today. I have taken a job in education and wonder how many lives I have impacted and how many of those students have gone on to work in a field where they are truly making a difference in this world.

The human connection and respect I have created with colleagues and students have been gifts I am truly grateful for and will cherish forever.

I have opened up a new possibility to create, innovate, and do something bigger. All of this has happened from a different arena and not always inside a classroom. These last few years, I have expanded my awareness to our current educational system and have been working to be open to new experiences and obtain new methods for delivering lessons and collaborating with my students.

CHAPTER TWELVE: CULTIVATING GRATITUDE

I am humbled by the feedback I have received and the new relationships I have made. I owe what my heart has been able to feel to my students, teachers, family, and coaches who have put up with my numerous ways to question theories and protocols again and again and go against the norms of certain things. I am extremely grateful for their encouragement and words of wisdom and allowing me to continue learning from them.

As I continue my teaching journey, I welcome new possibilities to connect with different leaders and the like. I hope you continue learning and growing as an individual and that you share your passions, talents, and knowledge with the world. I only hope I can do for my students what you all have done and continue to do for me.

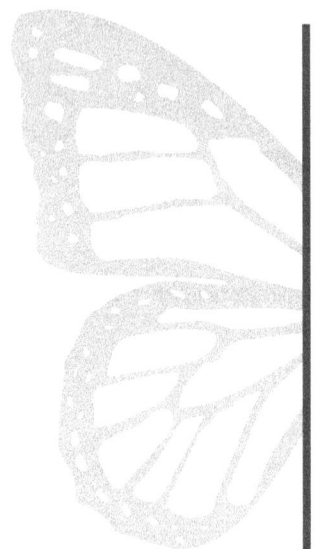

Acknowledgments

ACKNOWLEDGMENTS

I want to express a heartfelt gratitude to my parents, Salvador and Gloria Ramos. Because of you, I am the woman I am today. Dad, I know you are watching me from heaven, and I thank you for reminding me that I should never settle for less. Mom, you are my rock, and I am honored to be your daughter. I will always value the woman you have taught me to be, appreciate the lessons about life you taught me, and embrace the love you gave me.

My husband, Roger. I love you so much and appreciate all of your patience and understanding during this writing journey. Thank you for stopping everything to listen, love, and remind me that my dream of writing this book was closer than I imagined and that I needed to pursue it. I will always remember the three words you always said, "*Tu puedes campeona!*" At last it is complete. I adore you!

My siblings, Maribel Muñoz and Sal Ramos Jr., I love you both very much. Sister, I know you're smiling down from heaven and watching over me. You were the best role model and little sister an older sister can ask for. Phenomenal woman, that's you! Sal, thank you for being my first-round critic at everything and always giving me the best feedback whenever I needed a different point of view. Thank you for always making me laugh.

I want to thank my educational mentors from Montebello Unified and life-coaches who have shown me that I get to spread my wings and fly. Thank you for your constant reminders that I am flying through this world creating magical moments in life. I appreciate your guidance and ways you made me think about my vision and mission in life. Thank you for giving me the opportunity to learn from you.

ACKNOWLEDGMENTS

Thank you to my former teachers who have been an amazing inspiration and encouraged me to strive to do better in school and in life. Your words mean a great deal to me. I followed your educational path and began my own teaching journey. I will always remember life inside Mr. Anderson's fourth-grade class. To my softball coaches from Schurr High School, you were excellent guides for me—a young and mischievous teen who learned that the mindset on the field carried over to a productive mindset.

To my colleagues from Suva Elementary, thank you for all of the support you gave me during my difficult moments in my teaching career. Special thanks to Aida Hinojosa, for always making yourself available to listen and provide support for me during my early years of teaching. Your warmth and loving ways are infectious. Gracias, and I hope you are enjoying your retirement.

To those who are pursuing a career in education or working with children, I give you my sincere thanks because it takes a courageous, passionate, and patient person to teach and make a difference in the lives of others. Be the change, make great things happen! To teach is to touch a life forever!

To everyone who contributed or inspired *The Core of Teaching* to be written, this wouldn't be possible without you. My former student, Anthony Flores, your words were exactly what I needed to hear to start my writing journey. I am honored to have been your teacher.

Special thanks to my writing coach, Azul Terronez, and the entire Authors Who Lead Team. I could not have accomplished this without you. I shook the apples from the tree, emptied my head, and gave my book its voice. Thank you! You are all inspiring, and I am grateful for all of you.

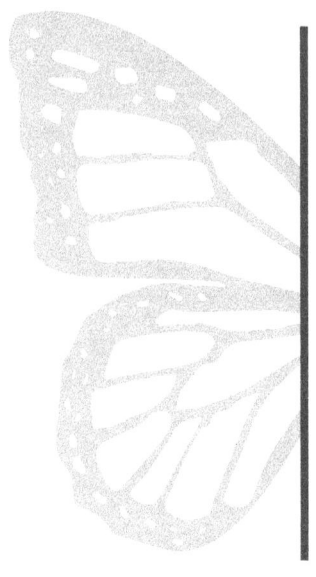

About the Author

Leticia Ramos

ABOUT THE AUTHOR

Leticia Ramos is an elementary school teacher who is passionate about working with children and creating extraordinary learning opportunities for students.

She has spent the last ten years working with educational leaders in developing leadership trainings for children and teens. After obtaining her certification through Jack Canfield's Train the Trainer Success Principles, she was inspired to pursue new endeavors in education, engage in personal development trainings, and grow her real estate business.

Leticia is passionate about promoting Growth Mindset habits and mindfulness practices with her students and understands that all students deserve opportunities to expand their intellect through different learning platforms.

One of Leticia's greatest joys is spending time with her family and traveling around the world. It excites her to be immersed in different cultures and she loves to expand her awareness about how people live, learn, and connect with each other. Connecting with like-minded leaders is something she thrives on and emphasizes that more people should study the art of observing their surroundings while being cognizant of the present.

Her time and experiences in the classroom have allowed her to be inspired by her previous teachers, mentors, and students. These people have changed her outlook on how she should teach and focus on purposeful and meaningful practices that allow you to find your true passion in life.

Leticia is committed to increasing student success and providing support to educators around the world in understanding *who* they are as teachers and *why* they love teaching!

www.ingramcontent.com/pod-product-compliance
Lightning Source LLC
LaVergne TN
LVHW041547070426
835507LV00011B/969